Language Guides

Choosing and using books in the first school
Editor: Dr Joyce M. Morris

7

Language Guides

Choosing and using books in the first school

Peggy Heeks
Assistant County Librarian
Berkshire

Macmillan Education

First published 1981

First published by
MACMILLAN EDUCATION LTD
London and Basingstoke
Associated companies and representatives
throughout the world

Filmset by Vantage Photosetting Co. Ltd.
Southampton and London

Printed in Hong Kong

ISBN 0 333 27309 5 HC

ISBN 0 333 32645 8 Ppr

Contents

ACKNOWLEDGEMENTS   vii

INTRODUCTION   ix

1   Adult hopes and children's needs   1

2   Playing with words   13

3   Interpreting pictures   29

4   What's in a story?   47

5   Traditional tales   71

6   Finding the facts   85

7   Organizing for use   108

8   Encouragements to reading   119

9   Storytelling   127

10   Beyond school   138

Acknowledgements

This book draws on experience gained in Berkshire, particularly through study groups and in-service sessions. I am grateful to my authority for the work opportunities afforded, and to colleagues engaged in education and library services for their insights.

Introduction

Writers, artists and publishers have collectively provided a vast and varied stock of books for young children. Potentially, this is already sufficient to meet the reading needs of at least every English-speaking child throughout the vital early years of schooling. In consequence, although a few important gaps need to be filled and, generally, new books of quality are to be welcomed, book provision is no longer largely a question of availability but of teachers knowing what is available. It is then a question of careful selection and effective use according to clearly-defined objectives.

These issues would be important at any time. They are crucial when book allowances are restricted. Teachers of the under-nines are well aware of this. Understandably, however, many are overwhelmed by the enormous task of getting to know what books are available to meet their pupils' needs. It is difficult enough to keep track of the innovatory reading/language schemes they could choose to use when funds permit. It is well-nigh impossible to study all the publications classified broadly as 'children's literature' and 'information' books. So what can be done to guard against haphazard, wasteful ways of choosing and using books?

This essentially practical guide provides some of the answers. In other words, it offers constructive suggestions for thought and action which have been put to good effect in various nursery, infant and first schools. These come from the author's experience of working closely with practising teachers, college tutors and fellow librarians. They also stem from her extensive knowledge as an internationally-recognised expert in the world of children's books.

Like the Bullock Committee, Peggy Heeks believes that it is absolutely essential for the staff of each school to collaborate in forming a book policy with agreed objectives. Therefore, she starts by highlighting the main factors which should be taken into account when building such a policy. These include detailed consideration of the role of books in personal development, transmitting a cultural heritage and promoting growth in reading and related language skills.

In the first chapter, the author adopts a scholarly, thoughtful and

inspirational approach to illuminate different views of child development through books. In subsequent chapters, she manages success-
fully to combine this approach with a very practical one. Thus, except
for basic reading schemes which were not part of her brief, she covers
in flexible style all that is necessary for teachers to know and be able to
do in order to operate an effective book policy.

The comprehensive range of topics covered in the text is clearly
indicated by the chapter headings and sub-headings. As this is a very
'meaty' guide, not to be digested all at one sitting, it is suggested that
teachers might like to begin with Chapter 9 which offers excellent
advice on storytelling. It might then be a good idea to turn to the
stimulating discussion of traditional tales in Chapter 5 as this forms a
natural link with the introductory chapter. After that, as a prelude to
detailed study, the guide should be read right through to get a feel for
its scope and direction.

At the end of each chapter, Peggy Heeks has provided a rich
abundance of readily-accessible information in the form of annotated
booklists, selection aids and other sources of help. She also gives
suggestions for workshop comparisons of children's books including
publications in the recently-expanded field of non-fiction. These
workshop ideas are one of the outstanding features of this guide, and
an example of the invaluable assistance it offers. Moreover, they
reflect the author's belief that 'the best guide to selection is one's own
judgement, trained through exercise and discussion, and backed by a
sense of purpose'.

Certainly, good judgement is exercised by those who select this
language guide to help them in their work with young children. It is
designed primarily for practising teachers not as a blueprint for
classroom adoption but as a comprehensive aid to their discussions
and the making of important decisions. It will obviously be of great
assistance to them, to teachers in training and their tutors, as well as to
librarians engaged in offering services to education. In short, *Choosing
and Using Books in the First School* is a wonderful resource for all
concerned with educating the minds and hearts of young children
through books.

JOYCE M. MORRIS

February 1981

I

Adult hopes and children's needs

Contents

A book policy
Adult hopes
Children's needs

Memories of childhood
Case studies
References

In the field of children's books and reading, we are at a point of discontent and discovery. We have passed through a decade or more of great activity in building up school book collections. The aim has been to ensure that children are 'surrounded by books'. Inspired by that key phrase, we have placed books in corridors, books in lobbies, books on window-ledges and in halls, believing accessibility to be the key factor in encouraging reading. Now we are beginning to examine the results of all this activity, and to question the assumptions behind it. This reassessment is made even more urgent by the current economic climate and the rising cost of book provision.

A book policy

Clearly, if children are to gain the maximum benefit from books, their teachers need a new precision in defining hopes. As early as 1966 Joyce Morris drew attention to this need in *Standards and Progress in Reading*[1]. The Bullock Report[2] made the same point in recommending that every 'primary school should have a book policy that reflects a set of objectives understood and accepted by the staff'. The message was reinforced by the 1972 report, *The Trend of Reading Standards*[3] and given a new perspective by Joan Tough's suggestions on language appraisal in *Listening to Children Talking*[4]. It accords with a desire among both professionals and the public for a clearer articulation of educational aims and, where feasible, a system of monitoring and evaluation.

Faith in the power of books to effect some kind of transformation just by their presence is diminishing because it has not produced the results claimed. Moreover, it now seems a rather haphazard system for professionals. Bullock was only articulating a general dissatisfaction in suggesting that action must be preceded by policy. This policy-building can take many different starting points, some of which are reviewed in this chapter. To be most effective the task should be carried out by each school staff working collaboratively, but education advisers and librarians can be brought in to assist. Some of the ideas can be considered in study groups based on Teachers' Centres. Although individual teachers may feel isolated or diffident, in any local education authority, there will always be some source of advice about ways of starting discussion of the subject.

Adult hopes

Adults have long had hopes about the beneficial effects of reading on human behaviour. In didactic verse and story, they have set out to teach children subjects as various as table manners, personal hygiene, fear of God, respect for truth and kindness to animals. More recently, belief in the power of the printed word has been demonstrated by those working to impede sexual stereotyping, foster racial harmony and spread understanding of the disadvantaged.

The effectiveness and appropriateness of this method of persuasion and the role of children's books in promoting sociological views are matters of controversy. Therefore, it is important to talk through these questions with colleagues when building up the book policy advocated by Bullock.

In this connection it will be helpful to read some of the documents emanating from the Children's Rights Workshop Project[5] and the Campaign to Impede Sex Stereotyping in the Young (CISSY)[6]. It will also be useful to study the views of writers who argue that books exert their influences in more subtle and less predictable ways. Among these are Sheila Egoff in *Only Connect*[7], Janet Hill in *Children are People*[8] and Kornei Chukovsky in *From Two to Five*[9]. Janet Hill, for example, castigates the 'crude pinpointing of cause and effect which becomes utterly ludicrous', while Chukovsky attacks judgment of a literary form in terms of social good as 'a pernicious method of criticism' based on 'repressive dogmas'.

Teachers are likely to be most concerned with the educational value of any children's book. Their hopes of the advantages to be gained from reading have tended to differ from those of the social campaigners. They can be summed up in the trilogy offered by John Dixon in *Growth through English*[10] under the headings 'skills', 'cultural heritage' and 'personal development'. While Dixon dismissed the first two models as too restrictive it is sensible, especially in view of changes in thinking since his book was first published in 1967, to consider the claims of all three to feature in a book policy.

Skills

Clearly, one of the major aims of First School teachers is to assist children to that mastery of basic reading skills which we now recognise as fundamental to educational attainment. Books are of obvious importance here, being a source of motivation for learning to read, a means of acquiring skills and of practising them. Books are also the tools for extending reading ability beyond the decoding stage.

In recent years, there has been a significant development in identifying a wide range of reading strategies and sub-skills, and in helping children acquire flexible reading speeds, comprehension techniques and study skills. Learning to read is seen as a process, a life-long pursuit, begun not ended when decoding has been mastered. While pupils in First Schools will, in general, be occupied with elementary stages, their teachers need to have an understanding of reading progression and slant their work accordingly.

Perception of reading as much more than a decoding technique is shared by many educationists who support this view of a process which begins with reading the lines, then moves to reading between the lines and finally beyond them. One recalls Thorndike's classic article 'Reading as reasoning'[11], I.A. Richard's phrase 'How to reap a page'[12], and Cliff Moon's description of reading as 'an active dialogue with a text'[13]. The Bullock Report[14] supports this attitude, setting out three major stages as follows:

A response to graphic signals in terms of the words they represent.	A response to text in terms of the meanings the author intended to set down.	A response to the author's meanings in terms of all the relevant previous experience and present judgments of the reader.

Even in the First School teachers need to be aware, beyond the minimum levels of literacy, of the possibilities of reading as a continued exploration of experience.

However we define reading, discussing it in isolation seems increasingly misleading. Today we are more likely to think in terms of language rather than reading skills, and to see the unity of that quartet, listening, speaking, reading, writing. We feel easier talking of the role of books in fostering language development than of their value in improving reading skills. Many influences have contributed to this change of emphasis which places reading in the context of language development and language development in the context of mental and social growth. Piaget did pioneer work in setting out the stages by which children master the process of reasoning and demonstrated the importance of this growth to linguistic ability. James Britton[15] linked language development with children's understanding of the outer world. 'If we recognise that we proceed in life through making a representation of reality and reacting to that, and that the primary task of speech is symbolisation of reality rather than communication, we can see how fundamental is the role language plays in our lives.' Joyce Morris[16] found that 'unsatisfactory language development is associated with inferior reading ability', and success or failure in reading has been shown as closely related to success or failure in the entire educational career of the child. Vygotsky[17] concluded that thought is not only expressed in words but comes into action through them. Our mental processes are developed by means of language and according to our linguistic ability.

The concensus is clear. As the Plowden Report[18] acknowledged, 'the development of language is central to the educational process'. Since books are obviously important tools in the acquisition of language facility, we need to pay serious attention to the skills model when building up a book policy, even though we may wish to give it a more modern title. This model need in no way be confined to 'minor elements of the total process' as John Dixon argued in his attack on concentration on skills. Recent statistics of adult illiteracy and of non-readers in secondary schools must serve to emphasize the importance of promoting reading fluency in the First School. Without that fluency the other benefits of reading are unlikely to accrue. As Sterl Artley[19] put it: 'Growth *through* reading is the ultimate goal . . ., while growth *in* reading is the means to that end'.

Cultural heritage

The second model identified by John Dixon stressed cultural heritage. Here the focus is on great literature and on ways of ensuring that children are introduced to such works as part of their inheritance. This model, too, Dixon dismissed as too limiting, partly because it is based on the idea of culture as something given *to* pupils rather than developed *by* them; partly because it 'confirmed the average teacher in his attention to the written word . . . as against the spoken word'. Again, one is bound to feel that it is Dixon who is being restrictive in his interpretation. There is, for example, no reason why the spoken word should not feature strongly in a programme planned around the cultural model. Nor is there any reason why this model should be regarded as a relic of the past, irrelevant today. Indeed, it can help us towards that promotion of a multi-ethnic community which is a topical concern, by making us aware of the background of legends, customs and arts contributing to its richness.

Personal development

The belief that books in general, and literature in particular, aid personal development permeated the Dartmouth Seminar reported in *Growth through English*[20]. One may trace this belief back to earlier centuries and in modern times especially to the teaching of F. R. Leavis, which influenced a generation of English specialists. It is still strong today. Group after group of teachers, when discussing book policy, will speak of the value of books in helping children understand themselves and other people. Through books children confront feelings and situations similar to their own, and meet characters and events which are completely new: both the confirmation and extension of experience contribute to their growth. Although much of the comment available refers to work in the Secondary School, it is equally applicable to the First School. As Joan Cass concluded, in her seminal book *Literature and the Young Child*[21] 'even at this stage, without realising it, children will, perhaps unconsciously acquire certain fundamental feelings in regard to literature and life'.

Bullock confirms the personal development model as standard: 'In Britain the tradition of literature teaching is one which aims at personal and moral growth, and in the last two decades this emphasis has grown'. Some of the implications of this attitude are explored in Chapter 4. What one needs to bear in mind here is that there are some dissenting views. Artley[22] has pointed out that there are no precise measures of the effect of books, while C. S. Lewis[23] has shown the earnest reader seeking self-improvement as a ridiculous figure far removed from reality: 'He is like the man who plays football to get exercise rather than to enjoy the game'.

Undoubtedly there have been some extravagant claims about the power of books to shape personalities and to civilize and sensitize human beings. Often such claims ignore the influence of direct experience, or the inter-play of first-hand and literary impressions. One begins to mistrust those who suggest that the effect of a book can be plotted exactly. Ironically, in view of the secondary bias in most of these discussions, it is probably in the First School that the link between books and personal development is most clear. Graham Greene[24] has suggested that at this impressionable age 'all books are books of divination', and Peter Hollindale[25] saw the early encounters with books 'an experience which may be critical in shaping a personality'. On this issue, which attracts a wide range of opinion, each teacher must reach his own conclusion, preferably in the context of staffroom or in-service discussion.

Perhaps our dissatisfaction with the narrow view that the 'good' book is one which 'positively makes for moral and emotional growth' arises from the greater understanding of the learning process which has developed over the last few years. Ronald Morris[26] is one of those who has helped us realise that through learning to read children begin to see themselves as learners and this has implications for their all-round development. Even earlier William Gray[27] reported on the strong correlation between social participation and reading ability and identified a reading/growing/reading/growing process which was self-generating. We perceive, too, that many books which are not 'good' in literary terms can be of great benefit to the reader. Books far from the award-winning circuit may be the springboards which suddenly change a reluctant reader to a committed one, enable a child to turn an image of reading failure to one of reading success, or offer a therapy unguessed by adults. Elaine Moss[28] provided an illustration in an article about her daughter's favourite book, *Peppermint*, a book 'totally without distinction', yet precious to Alison and important to her development. The anecdote reminds us that adult hopes need to be tempered by common sense and observation of actual children. It also suggests that an equally valid starting point for the exercise of building up a book policy would be consideration of children's developmental needs and the ways in which books meet them.

Children's needs

There is no blueprint we can turn to for an analysis of children's needs and the books appropriate to them. This is fortunate in as much as it would provide no room for fresh thought on the many new children's books published each year. As things stand, each teacher or group of teachers has to consider relationships between development and reading, reaching individual conclusions, and leaving the way open for continuing reassessment. Works like Isaacs's *The Children we Teach*[29], Piaget's *The Child's Conception of the World*[30], or Olson's *Child Development*[31] provide a necessary background to our own observations. We learn from them the particular importance of the years from four to eight in building up basic structures of thought. The child moves from a stage when ideas of space, time, measurement etc are in a flux, and he is continually reorganizing his internal model of the world. He moves to a stage when he can use many adult thought-processes and his picture of the world is more constant – in technical terms, the level of conservation and concrete operations. He also moves from a time of emotional storms and complexities to a period of relative tranquillity.

The emotional range of the young child is, indeed, considerable, yet both the range and strength of these emotions are often overlooked or dismissed by adults. Fear, guilt and aggression are all to be found through the nursery and infant years. Loneliness is as keen a problem for young children trying to find a place in the group structure as it is for the elderly. The desire for individual recognition and achievement are as clear in the First School as in adolescence. It is in the First School that the feeling of individual helplessness is at its sharpest. These emotional needs can be categorized in many ways, but any grouping is likely to distinguish two basic needs from which the others proceed. These are the needs for security and experience or, to use the terms of Sebesta and Wallen[32], 'sanctuary and knowledge'. It is perhaps true that these are life-long needs, given different emphases at varying ages or stages: it is certainly true that these are particularly apparent in the early years of childhood.

The young child is a stranger in an adult world, where the terms of reference are by no means clear. One of his first tasks is to try to make sense of this puzzling environment. One finds many comic mistakes made as young children attempt to strengthen their understanding of everyday phenomena. For example, Chukovsky tells of the little girl who watered a puppy to make him grow after watching mother watering the flowers; of the small boy closing his eyes to make night-time; and of the ceaseless questioning characteristic of this stage such as 'Where does the smoke fly?' 'How did the moon happen?' 'Who rocks the trees?' We may find similar examples from our own experience, all demonstrating the child's struggle to get his bearings in life.

One can find a significantly close relationship between the developmental needs of First School children and the books available to them. The earliest books often do little more than portray children on their small domestic round, as they go to the shops, play with toys, or help mother. Characteristic themes are the first day at school, a family outing, or the start of friendships. All serve to reinforce children's understanding of their own environment and so promote a sense of security. As young children are extremely egocentric these little documentaries both support their self image and move them to an interest in other people. Exploring these books, seeing others in situations similar to their own, children can begin to lose their sense of separateness. They learn that most reassuring truth: 'It happens to other people too'. Stories of small achievements or of discouragements overcome diminish young children's feelings of helplessness and strengthen belief in their ability to succeed.

Once a sound base in the real world has been established, children can move out from that security to fresh experience. Here will come the time for fantasies, for adventures set in other places or times, for stories which touch on fear or other emotions still only half-understood. Factual books have an important part to play here in extending experience and satisfying curiosity. A book policy which starts from consideration of children's developmental needs will seek to find a range of books which remind the child of his past, keep pace with his present, and touch on what he may become. Some specific titles will be discussed in later chapters: the point to note here is that one should seek to offer works which in content, presentation, and level of difficulty reassure the child about his mastery of the immediate environment and also those which widen his view of the possibilities of life.

Memories of childhood

Our hopes as educationists and our theories of child development need to be tempered with observations of real children. For all of us, the child we know best is the child each used to be. In trying to establish what books can do for today's children it is salutary to think back to the impact books had on us in childhood. It is not an easy task. Just as past landscapes become hazed over with perpetual sunshine so, too, do early encounters with books. We tend to forget the difficulties of print, or the banal books. The longeurs fall away and we are left remembering the insights into human behaviour gained mourning for home with Mole, daring with Emil or sympathizing with Eeyore. All such memories may be true and necessary to our adult belief in the role of books for personal development, but they miss out important aspects of our first meeting with print.

The quotations below offer a different perspective. They were gathered from a teachers' study group and a similar exercise might well form part of any school's process of formulating a book policy.

1 'My first memories of books are mixed up with those of furniture. The hard, slippery couch where strange uncles read comics to me, the hassock under the dining room table where, hidden by the chenille tablecloth, I "read" Punch, turning over the pages and laughing as I had seen grown-ups do. I didn't understand the pictures or the text: the pleasure was in carrying out an adult activity.'

2 'On good days my mother would prop me against her in an armchair and read to me. I can't remember her voice, or expression, or much about the stories, except my favourite, *The Pie and the Pattypan*. But reading then was made up of closeness, cosiness, and good humour.'

3 'I can't remember the stories in my first books, only the smell and texture. The stiff, brittle leaves of the Beatrix Potter books, always smelling a little inky; the smudgy pictures on soft paper of the comics;

the thick blotting-paper feel of the Christmas annuals. I loved going to the shop once a week on the same day for my special comic: it always seemed as if it had been made specially for me.'

4 'I chose books mainly for their shape. The tiny size of the Reverend Awdry books and Beatrix Potter stories made them like personal and secret possessions. The large flat books made me feel grown-up and important. When I graduated to ordinary-sized books I was very fussy about the page layout. I never knew *what* I was looking for, but I always knew when the size or spacing of type were right. It didn't seem to matter what the book was about as long as its looks pleased me.'

These comments from teachers searching out their memories of childhood emphasize the importance of things quite other than book content. In establishing a book policy regard should be paid to the features which come to the fore here: the setting for reading; the adult presence; the status of reading as a prestige activity; the book as physical object.

Case studies

The searching of our own memories needs complementing by observations of today's children. Our theories must match the reality of the children we teach and be continuously tested against their needs, tastes and responses. A book policy is not something worked out once and for all but needs to be open to adjustment as fresh understanding comes from our own work and from the research studies of others. Practitioners have an important role to play here, for there is amazingly little research information about reading growth and patterns. Teachers are in an admirable position to illuminate this area by the simple recording of books read, by comparative studies or occasional long discussions and by book-based projects. There are many surveys of reading interests based on questions such as 'Which books have you read during the last month?'. The methodology is notoriously inadequate, assuming in children a precise time-concept and a better memory for authors and titles than adults possess. It is small wonder that *Little Women, Treasure Island* and similar famous classics usually top the list in such polls.

The last major English survey, reported in *Children and their Books*[33], used this basis and included a list of similar researches. It also identified a need to move on to longitudinal studies. Frank Whitehead, who led this research project, drew attention to the uniqueness of each child's reading-personality and of 'the need consequently to study it in the context of the child's temperament, interests, attitudes and total life-situation'. He proposed longitudinal studies of a much smaller number of children, following their reading over a period of years and establishing 'the specific determining influences, whether in home, neighbourhood or school, that effect changes in children's reading habits and tastes'. First Schools could help fill this information gap by studying the reading patterns of children as they progress through the school, while class teachers could make a significant contribution by collecting data on the books read over one school year by one class or by selected children within it.

Of the longitudinal studies which exist, most were written by parents and cover pre-school years. A pioneer survey, still well worth reading by First School teachers, is Dorothy Neal White's *Books before Five*[34]. As a former children's librarian, Mrs White was well-qualified to select appropriate books for her daughter, but even she was surprised by the vehemence of affection shown for certain books and the disregard of some of her own favourites. This account of what books meant to Carol in the nursery years is a testament to the inter-relationship of life and literature. The books extended her apprehension of direct experience while, in turn, Carol's direct experiences enriched her understanding of the stories.

A more recent study of a young child's reaction to books is *Cushla and her Books* by Dorothy Butler[35]. Cushla was a severely handicapped child, with specific physical deformities and some general retardation. Her parents were determined to reduce the effect of these disabilities as much as possible, and the book reflects their devotion and sensitivity to their child. It also demonstrates the power of books for individual development in a fresh and immediate way, and the vital role played by adults 'prepared to intercede' in the process of linking children and books. Dorothy Butler's account begins with Cushla, her granddaughter, being introduced to books at four months old and ends with her just before her fourth birthday, settling on the sofa with her rag doll and a pile of books. 'Now I can read to Looby Lou, 'cause she's tired and sad, and she needs a cuddle and a bottle and a book.' As many of Cushla's books were stories regularly provided in First Schools, her reaction to them provides insights to colour not only work with other handicapped children but with normal pupils.

Margaret Clark's *Young Fluent Readers*[36] takes a different perspective. It is not an account of one child's encounters with books, but a study of the progress of 32 children who were already reading fluently when they started school. The author thought it would be illuminating to look at the conditions which make for reading success, and with this in mind analysed the personal characteristics of these children, their approach to learning, family background and favourite books. The findings have interest for all concerned with children's reading, whether as parents, teachers or librarians.

Some of Margaret Clark's conclusions on reading environment will be referred to in Chapter 7. The point to note here is the great variety of reading tastes and habits found in the group. We often describe books as 'Suitable for reception classes' or 'Just right for top Infants'. *Young Fluent Readers* is a deterrent to such stereotyping. The reading diaries kept by these children when 7 – 8 years old include entries for books we would be unlikely to link with this age band. Included are *Robinson Crusoe, Treasure Island, Black Beauty* – even *Jane Eyre* and Burns' poetry. In framing a book policy it is easy to get too theoretical. Reports such as Margaret Clark's have a special value in offering observation of real children to offset the more academic books on the reading process.

References

1. Morris, J.M. *Standards and Progress in Reading* (Slough [Berks], National Foundation for Educational Research 1966)
2. Department of Education & Science *A Language for Life*, Bullock Report (HMSO 1975)
3. Start, K.B. & Wells, B.K. *The Trend of Reading Standards* (Slough [Berks], National Foundation for Educational Research 1972)
4. Tough, J. *Listening to Children Talking* (Ward Lock Educational 1976)
5. Children's Rights Workshop Book Project, 4 Aldebert Terrace, London SW8
6. CISSY, c/o 24 Cressida Road, London N19
7. Egoff, S. *and others. Only Connect* (New York, Oxford University Press 1969)
8. Hill, J. *Children are People* (H. Hamilton 1973)
9. Chukovsky, K. *From Two to Five* (Berkeley, University of California Press; Cambridge University Press 1968)
10. Dixon, J. *Growth through English* (Oxford University Press for the National Association for the Teaching of English 1967)
11. Thorndike, E.L 'Reading as reasoning', *Journal of Educational Psychology*, 8 (1917), 323 – 32
12. Richards, I.A. *How to Read a Page* (Routledge 1943)
13. Moon, C. *Individualised Reading* 5th edn (Reading [Berks], University of Reading, Centre for the Teaching of Reading, 1975)
14. *op. cit.*[2]
15. Britton, J. *Language and Learning* (Penguin Books 1972)
16. *op. cit.*[1]
17. Vygotsky, L. S. *Thought and Language* (Boston, Massachusetts Institute of Technology Press & Wiley 1962)
18. Department of Education & Science *Children and their Primary Schools* Plowden Report (HMSO 1967)
19. Artley, S. 'But skills are not enough', *Education*, 79 (1959), 542
20. *op. cit.*[10]
21. Cass, J. *Literature and the Young Child* (Longman 1967)
22. *op. cit.*[19]
23. Lewis, C.S. *An Experiment in Criticism* (Cambridge University Press 1961)
24. Greene, G. *The Lost Childhood and Other Essays* (Eyre & Spottiswoode 1951)
25. Hollindale, P. *Choosing Books for Children* (Elek 1974)
26. Morris, R. 'What children learn in learning to read', *English in Education*, 5 Winter (1971), 8 – 19
27. Gray, W.S. & Rogers, B. *Maturity in Reading: its Nature and Appraisal* (Chicago, University of Chicago Press 1956)
28. Moss, E. 'The Peppermint lesson', *Books*, 2 Winter (1970), 22 – 3

29. Isaacs, S. *The Children We Teach* (University of London Press 1932)
30. Piaget, J. *The Child's Conception of the World* (Routledge 1929)
31. Olson, W.C. *Child Development* 2nd edn (Boston, D.C. Heath 1959)
32. Sebesta S. & Wallen, C. *The First R: Readings on Teaching Reading* (Science Research Associates 1972)
33. Whitehead, F. *and others. Children and their Books* (Macmillan 1977)
34. White, D.N. *Books before Five* (New Zealand Council for Educational Research 1954)
35. Butler, D. *Cushla and her Books* (Hodder & Stoughton 1979)
36. Clark, M. *Young Fluent Readers* (Heinemann Educational 1976)

2

Playing with words

Contents

First encounters   The teacher's role
Nursery rhymes   References
Nonsense verse   Booklist
Poetry

First encounters

'We didn't understand the words but we understood the play' was the comment of a group of teenagers taken to see *Romeo and Juliet*. There is a similarity with children's first approaches to language. They understand the meaning but not the words. The sharp urgency of 'No', the soothing rhythm of a lullaby, the teasing changes of pace in rhyming games all have an impact on toddlers long before they possess an orthodox vocabulary. Even at this early stage children enjoy playing with sounds, experimenting with language and savouring its satisfactions. The imitative instinct is strong, and the tone of quite long adult speech patterns will be reproduced, albeit with no words we understand. Once a 'real' word has been learnt it will be pronounced repeatedly with relish and a great sense of pride. There is a sensuous delight in the production of sounds, in the explosive lip noises of *p* and *b*, the drumming of *d*, and in the buzzing, hissing, sibilant sounds of *s*, *z*, *ch*, and *sh*. Added to this is a musical pleasure when rhymes are spoken or chanted.

This response to words is quite spontaneous, a natural reaction at a time when children are largely outside the influence of educationists. It is a child-centred pleasure, not an adult-imposed one. This factor is of considerable significance to our approach to language in the First School. So, too, is the way in which the pleasure is usually enhanced by an adult presence. While this kind of language use arises from delight in utterance rather than a desire to communicate, children like to have someone on whom to practise the effects of language, someone to whom to demonstrate the interesting new sound combinations they have invented.

The language characteristics of children just beginning to establish speech continue throughout the pre-school years. Chukovsky[1] has called the child in these years before five 'a linguistic genius, who remembers, imitates and creates, moving from a vocabulary of around 250 words at two years to one of several thousand by three, and to quite a good mastery of linguistic structures'. Even the inventions which are a feature of this age-group are based on logical extensions of accepted phrases or ideas. 'Look' says the three-year-old in the bath 'now I'm barefoot all over'. Combing her hair before the mirror she explains, 'I'm just pretty-miring myself'. Chukovsky gives many examples of children's creative use of words and most of us could corroborate and add to them from our own observations.

We have already noted the child's need to make sense of his surroundings, and his use of classification to help in the task. A similar process of grouping 'like with like' can be seen in encounters with words. At quite an early stage children will enjoy simple rhyming or pairing games.

'Who's on the stair? No one is there' or

'I'm having fun, eating a bun'.

It is interesting that many of the first words toddlers speak consist of paired syllables – Dad-dad; Ma-ma; Bye-bye; Night-night. The same desire for repetition can be seen in the poetry children make up, as the following examples of a four-year-old's verse from *Children Using Language* show.[2]

'She met a little mouse
She met a little mouse
She met a little mouse
How do you do little mouse
Won't you come in, little mouse?
In my playroom?
And well and well and well
Little mouse said
Oh yes! Oh yes! Oh yes! . . .'

Along with this rhyming play comes an appreciation of the ridiculous.

'I've lost my spoon. It turned into a balloon' or

'Here's your dinner. It will make you thinner'.

The pattern continues into the First School years. There, too, we can observe an instinctive pleasure in sounds and rhythms, an enjoyment of repetition, and the value of an audience. We can see an important part for adults in sharing and extending these enjoyments, and in building an environment of encouragement and security in which children's own efforts can prosper.

Nursery rhymes

When we examine the anthologies recommended for young children we see how closely the material there matches the child's early delight in words. Many of the first rhymes we share with children have an added element of play, combining movement and rhythm, and uniting adult and child in an individual relationship. Perhaps first will come finger rhymes like 'Hickory, Dickory, Dock' or 'Dance, Thumbkin, dance', and jogging rhymes: 'To market, to market, to buy a plum bun'; 'This is the way the ladies ride' or gentler rocking rhymes like 'See-saw Margery Daw'. Extensions of these are the games to be played by a number of children, of which 'Oranges and lemons' and 'Here we go round the mulberry bush' are the best known.

Other nursery rhymes can be used to build on the pleasure in sounds and invention which we have noted as characteristic of young children. Of such kind are 'Peter, Peter, pumpkin eater'; 'Deedle deedle dumpling, my son John'; 'Hickety, pickety, my black hen'. Many are so rhythmical that we turn to chanting or singing them:

'Cock a doodle doo,
My dame has lost her shoe' or

'Girls and boys come out to play,
The moon doth shine as bright as day'.

Some have the internal pairing of rhymes seen in children's own verse:

'Fire! Fire! said Mrs Dyer;
Where? Where? said Mrs Dare;
Up the town, said Mrs Brown;
Any damage? said Mrs Gamage;
None at all, said Mrs Hall.'

From these children will move on to tongue twisters like 'She sells sea shells' and 'Betty Botter bought some butter'. They will also enjoy solving and asking riddles such as:

'As red as an apple, as round as a ball,
Higher than the steeple, weathercock and all' or

'Two brothers we are,
Great burdens we bear,
On which we are bitterly pressed;
The truth is to say,
We are full all the day,
And empty when we go to rest'.

Nursery rhymes are sometimes dismissed as archaic or irrelevant in content but many, in fact, are full of earthly wisdom and shrewd observation, for example 'There was a little girl, and she had a little curl'; 'I love little pussy, her coat is so warm'; 'God made man and man makes money'; the tale of the accommodating Jack Sprat. Indeed, as we look through anthologies, the variety of the rhymes is the most striking feature. We have counting rhymes and alphabet sequences such as 'A was an Apple Pie'; 'A was an Archer', cumulative rhymes like 'This is the house that Jack built'; 'One old Oxford ox opening oysters', 'My grandfather died and he left me a cow'; narrative verse and commentary on old political issues. The title 'nursery rhymes' is in some sense a misnomer in its present association with the three to five age-group. Anyone looking through *The Oxford Nursery Rhyme Book*[3] will see that the contents can span the whole First School and beyond. Iona and Peter Opie, the experts in this field, have identified 150 well-known rhymes and several hundred previously neglected. Their *Oxford Nursery Rhyme Book* and *Puffin Book of Nursery Rhymes*[4] together contain some 1,000 rhymes. With such a wealth of material each teacher should be able to find something appropriate to a range of occasions and audiences.

Nursery rhymes have been recommend by the Bullock Report as a stimulus to language development and an aid in the task of sound differentiation. 'It is, of course, well known that children respond more than most adults to verbal play; what is not generally realised is that the language skills used in verbal play – repeating jingles, puns, riddles, matching rhymes etc. – may be very important in early reading.' Piaget has also pointed out that peer group culture is fostered by the existence of a large body of shared language and lore – a reminder that these rhymes are part of a cultural heritage which we have a responsibility to transmit. Their similarity in structure and free use of language to the rhymes children make up in street and playground rituals is striking, and suggests one reason for their immediate appeal. This attraction to nursery rhymes is by no means confined to English-speaking children. In *Word Play* Peter Farb[5] noted that 'children who speak unrelated languages also recite verses that apparently follow the same pattern as the English ones'. Chinese children's verse, for example, resembles our nursery verse in its content, its patterns of rhyme and rhythm, and its inclusion of nonsense elements. Similar kinds of verse have been found in Nigeria, Sumatra, and the South Pacific – an indication of its fundamental appeal.

Peter Farb set out at some length the function of poetry in any community, and analysed the creative pleasure which both children and adults get from playing with words. The value of expressive play elements in language development has been stressed by many leading educationists, among them James Britton[6], Michael Oakeshott[7] and

Patrick Creber[8], who attacked the very narrow range of language use encouraged in the average school environment. The 'efficient learning of a language depends upon our playing with it, savouring it, messing around with it'. As the Opies' book, *The Lore and Language of Schoolchildren*[9], makes clear, these are also natural and enjoyable activities.

Current enthusiasm for nursery rhymes is high, but it is only fair to note that there have been several occasions in the past when they have been regarded as a pernicious influence. In 1851, for example, Richard Henry Horne[10] wrote a long article on the dangers of these ancient rhymes. According to him, the majority encouraged children to unprincipled or wanton acts, witness the greed of Little Jack Horner, the thieving habits of Welshman Taffy and Tom the piper's son, and the violence to old people so heartlessly described in Goosey-Goosey Gander. Horne observed, 'it looks as if the great majority of those compositions have been the work of one or more of the wickedest of old witches ever heard of, and with the direct intention of perverting, if not destroying, the generosity, innocence, pure imagination and tender feelings of childhood at as early a stage as possible'. A hundred years later another critic, Geoffrey Handley-Taylor[11], produced a list of unsuitable elements in nursery rhymes including a case of body-snatching, and another of death by shrivelling.

Today it is often argued that nursery rhymes are lacking in 'relevance' (that much-worked word) to modern children. Again we come back to individual conviction and objectives. Teachers who spend time sharing nursery rhymes with their pupils should be able to present a reasoned case for doing so. They also have to decide which among the numerous versions available they will choose. Notes on some recommended editions are given at the end of this chapter, but Maurice Sendak's words[12] may serve here as a summary. 'Only Mother Goose, that doughty old wonder bird, could have survived the assiduous attention of generations of champions and detractors, illustrators and anthologists. More than merely survive, she has positively flourished – younger, fresher, and more superbly beautiful than ever . . .'

Nonsense verse

The boundaries between nursery rhymes, nonsense verse and children's poetry are blurred, with considerable overlap in content. The distinction is rather in origin. Nursery rhymes are part of an oral tradition and, as such, have been much changed over the years. Mothers and nurses altered the old rhymes to suit their tastes or the occasion, and replaced words or sections which they could not remember. The Opies[13] describe the rhymes as 'the true waifs of our literature in that their original wordings, as well as their authors, are usually unknown'. It is clear that many were unrelated snatches of adult jokes, political satire, popular songs and country maxims. In contrast, nonsense verse is a more recent form, dating largely from the nineteenth century, and generally made up for the express purpose of amusing children.

The outstanding exponent was, of course, Edward Lear whose *A Book of Nonsense* in 1846[14] came as a welcome robust contrast to the rather sentimental, pious verse then current, declaring by its very title that its sole purpose was to entertain. Today, verses like 'The Owl and the Pussycat went to Sea' and 'There was an Old Man with a Beard' are still among the most popular in Primary School classrooms. They are not tied to any one age-group. At each stage children can find something appealing in them, whether it be those amazing meals ('mince and slices of quince', taken with a runcible spoon), the felicitous phrasing, the sidelights on human frailty, or the juxtaposition of the familiar and the ridiculous. They are perfectly suited to reading aloud, having a simplicity and inevitability which give even the nervous reader a measure of confidence – witness the opening of a poem often regarded as among Lear's best:

> 'On the coast of Coromandel,
> Where the early pumpkins blow,
> In the middle of the woods,
> Lived the Yonghy Bonghy Bo.'

The problem for the teacher is likely to be not whether to use Lear, but which edition to use, for one has a choice of Lear's own original illustrations, the Edwardian drawings of Leslie Brooke, and a range of modern work, much of it in colour. Some suggestions are listed at the end of this chapter but readers wishing to look at this question in greater detail will find a helpful critical context in Crispin Fishers' 1969 article, 'A load of old nonsense'[15].

From Lear we move to Lewis Carroll, who may have read *A Book of Nonsense* as a boy, through many minor nineteenth century writers to A. A. Milne and contemporary figures such as Michael Baldwin, Ivor Cutler and Spike Milligan. Much of their work is particularly successful in Middle Schools but some of it is enjoyed in First Schools. While nonsense verse, by definition, may not have to be understood, a knowledge of normality is needed in order to realise the ridiculous elements. This is a form more sophisticated than one might suppose from its simple rhythms and structure, and the balance between underestimating and boring a First School audience is fine. Only personal taste and judgment can suggest the right time to introduce poems like Spike Milligan's *The ABC*[16]:

> ' 'Twas midnight in the schoolroom
> And every desk was shut,
> When suddenly from the alphabet
> Was heard a loud "Tut-tut!" . . .'

or Ogden Nash's *The Poultries*[17]:

> 'Let's think of eggs.
> They have no legs.
> Chickens come from eggs,
> But they have legs.
> The plot thickens:
> Eggs come from chickens,
> But have no legs under 'em.
> What a conundrum!'

Poetry

Nobody has yet satisfactorily resolved the basic problem: whether to define children's poetry as material written expressly for them, or as the wider range of material enjoyed by them. When the Opies came to select entries for *The Oxford Book of Children's Verse*[18] they found this the principal difficulty, being hard put to distinguish 'the verse that was always for children from that subsequently adopted for children'. Nor has anyone got much further with the associated puzzle of whether there is in fact such a thing as poetry for children or would light verse be a more appropriate term? These are not just the academic questions they seem, for anyone choosing poems to present in the classroom is involved in finding an answer. In the absence of certainties we can hope only for clues, and may find a starting point in the Bullock Report's encouragement of presentation by teachers of the widest selection of literature possible. Children have in their time claimed for themselves popular rhymes, tales of Robin Hood and King Arthur, and the adventures of Crusoe and Gulliver, all originally intended for adults. We need not, therefore, be surprised at their taking over Cowper's *John Gilpin*, Blake's *Song of Innocence* or lines heavy with mystery such as – 'The splendour falls on castle walls'; 'Full fathom five thy father lies'; 'If I should ever by chance grow rich' – all of which have an incantatory pleasure. As for the stature of poetry written directly for a child audience, it is true that much has a banal or tendentious quality, but we can also find work, such as that of Walter de la Mare, James Reeves or Charles Causley, which can claim judgment by literary standards.

Reminders of the early exhortatory tone of verse written for children remain in cautionary rhymes still popular today as for example in Belloc's 'Matilda told such dreadful lies' or Hoffmann's 'Augustus was a chubby lad'. But it would be doing children a disservice to limit them to work of a comic nature. Looking at three anthologies only, *The Oxford Book of Children's Verse*, *The Puffin Quartet of Poets*[19] and *The Puffin Book of Magic Verse*[20] one can find a wide emotional and subject range of entries accessible to First School children. Celebrations of the natural world, lullabies, charms, mysteries and character sketches are here, the consoling, the happy, the sad and the homely, representing experience in its most compressed literary form.

The teacher's role

Poetry can be a powerful agent in furthering the teacher's purposes. It builds on and extends children's great feeling for rhythm, it gives them a sense of a culture shared, and it offers insights and pleasures which increase confidence and understanding.

Ideally, children will come to school with some acquaintance with poetry. Many parents soon realise how useful nursery rhymes are in amusing and distracting children. They make the walk to the bus stop less tiring, waiting times less frustrating, bedtimes more bearable: they become part of the fabric of family life, not special occasion presentations. This approach may give a lead to teachers looking for ways to introduce poetry in the classroom. All kinds of situations and subjects will call to mind a particular poem which one wants to share. Children can be encouraged to suggest favourite or new rhymes they would like to hear and any story session can include some verse. Bullock notes that too often poetry is presented as something 'precious, arcane, to be revered', instead of as a form relevant to children's interests and ideas, speaking directly to them. There is a fallacious belief that poetry requires a special voice or style of delivery, a belief dispelled by the poets themselves who more often adopt a conversational rather than rhetorical style when reading their own work. The features to cultivate are a variety of approach and an expanding repertoire. Both children and teachers benefit from an element of surprise and release from the boredom of favourite college pieces grown stale with over-use.

Apart from hearing poems read aloud children should be exploring them alone, particularly in some of the simple picture-book versions. Later, as writing competence is established, children can copy rhymes they particularly like and make their personal anthologies. Sometimes the teacher can duplicate a range of poems and let pupils build up a booklet from them, illustrated with their own drawings.

Poetry is a very effective stimulus to creativity in the form of art, drama, music and children's own verse-making. Inevitably, the poetry children write will be influenced by the models presented to them. This is amply demonstrated in Sandy Brownjohn's practical guide *Does it have to rhyme?*[21] Jeremy Mulford has pointed out in *Children Using Language*[22] that too often what they give back are exercises in finding word rhymes rather than expressions of personal experience. It is clear that the teacher has a responsibility to show, through selection and presentation, that poetry is more than verbal dexterity. Crucial factors are the teacher's own attitude towards poetry and the kind of response from pupils that is encouraged. In the work of building a rich language environment, rhymes and poems are powerful aids. From them, in Michael Marland's phrase[23], 'whole possibilities of how words can be put together are absorbed'. From them too, as with all literature, we can become aware of something even more important; whole possibilities of how life can be experienced.

References

1. Chukovsky, K. *From Two to Five* (Berkeley, University of California Press: Cambridge University Press 1968)
2. Jones, A. & Mulford, J. (Ed) *Children Using Language: an Approach to English in the Primary School* (Oxford University Press for the National Association for the Teaching of English 1971)
3. Opie, I. & Opie, P. (Ed) *The Oxford Nursery Rhyme Book* (Oxford University Press 1955)
4. Opie, I. & Opie, P. (Ed) *The Puffin Book of Nursery Rhymes* (Penguin Books 1963)
5. Farb, P. *Word Play* (Cape 1974)
6. Britton, J. *Language and Learning* (Penguin Books 1972)
7. Oakeshott, M. *The Voice of Poetry in the Conversation of Mankind* (Bowes & Bowes 1959)
8. Creber, P. *Lost for Words: Language and Educational Failure* (Penguin Books in association with the National Association for the Teaching of English 1972)
9. Opie, I. & Opie, P. *The Lore and Language of Schoolchildren* (Oxford University Press 1959)
10. Horne, R.H. 'A witch in the nursery', *Household Words*, 78 (20 Sept 1851), 601–9
11. Handley-Taylor, G. 'A selected bibliography of literature relating to nursery rhyme reform', Manchester, *True Aim* (1952)
12. Sendak, M. 'Mother Goose's garnishings', *Book Week*, 5 (31 Oct 1965), 38–40
13. Opie, I. & Opie, P. (Ed) *The Oxford Dictionary of Nursery Rhymes* (Oxford University Press 1951)
14. Lear, E. *A Book of Nonsense* (Warne 1846)
15. Fisher, C. 'A load of old nonsense', *Growing Point*, 8 (Nov 1969), 1418–20
16. Milligan, S. 'The ABC' in Cole, W. *Oh, How Silly* (Methuen 1971)
17. Nash, O. 'The Poultries' in Cole, W. *Oh, That's Ridiculous* (Methuen 1972)
18. Opie, I. & Opie, P. (Ed) *The Oxford Book of Children's Verse* (Oxford University Press 1973)
19. Graham, I. (Ed) *The Puffin Quartet of Poets* (Puffin 1958)
20. Causley, C. (Ed) *The Puffin Book of Magic Verse* (Puffin 1974)
21. Brownjohn, S. *Does it have to rhyme?* (Hodder & Stoughton 1980)

22. *op. cit.* [2]
23. Marland M. (Ed) *Language Across the Curriculum* (Heinemann Educational 1977)

Booklist

Nursery rhymes

Standard collections

The Nursery Rhymes of England collected by James Orchard Halliwell
   (Bodley Head)
Originally published in 1842, this was the first large-scale collection
of nursery rhymes in this country. Over 700 rhymes are included,
divided into 18 groups according to type or subject, e.g. Jingles,
Local, Games, Paradoxes. Decorative black and white chapter headings are provided by Maureen Roffey. As this book is a scholarly
collection with a small number of illustrations and rather academic
format it is more suitable for staff reference than for children's use.
The Oxford Nursery Rhyme Book assembled by Iona and Peter Opie
   (Oxford University Press)
The fullest collection available, containing 800 items arranged in nine
sections with a progression from play-rhymes and lullabies to ballads,
riddles and sections which take on the tone of adult poetry. The book
has 600 illustrations drawn mainly from books of the eighteenth and
nineteenth centuries. It includes several of Thomas and John Be-
wick's engravings, supplemented by 150 specially-prepared scraper-
board designs by Joan Hassall. The compilers' view is that however
much 'a child's eye may momentarily be caught by a large flush of
colour, there is a particular pleasure in examining and re-examining
the precise miniature world of the Bewick-style engraving', and many
parents and teachers can support that view. The quaintness of the tiny
engravings provides a suitable accompaniment to these old rhymes.
The extent of the selection makes it an obvious source book for the
Primary School age-group.
The Puffin Book of Nursery Rhymes gathered by Iona and Peter Opie,
   with illustrations by Pauline Baynes (Puffin)
A collection authoritative in content and approachable in format,
containing some 200 items, including 150 standard rhymes. Arrange-
ment is by subject.
Lavender's Blue edited by Kathleen Lines, illustrated by Harold Jones
   (Oxford University Press)
A carefully-compiled section by a sensitive editor matched by illustra-
tions of high quality. There is a simplicity and clarity about Harold

Jones's water colours which is particularly fitted to these innocent verses, and the artist's care for page design is a constant source of satisfaction.

Current collections

The versions listed below indicate the continuing interest in nursery rhymes and the variety of valid approaches to their presentation.

Cakes and Custard children's rhymes chosen by Brian Alderson and
  illustrated by Helen Oxenbury (Heinemann)
A collection of rhymes, mainly traditional, characterised by the vigour of its approach and the wit of its illustrations. A book to dispel the idea that nursery rhymes belong to a genteel never-never land. The care for the pattern of text and pictures makes each page opening a fresh pleasure.

Nicola Bayley's Book of Nursery Rhymes (Cape)
Nicola Bayley is essentially a decorative artist, here weaving pretty borders and settings for some twenty well-known rhymes. This is the nursery rhyme land made familiar by Walter Crane and Leslie Brooke, presented with a degree of sophistication in carefully-patterned and detailed illustrations. The care given to page design is outstanding, and one sees why Nicola Bayley's books are collectors' items for adults.

The Great Big Book of Nursery Rhymes chosen by Peggy Blakeley with
  drawings by Frank Francis (Black)
A large colourful book with text in big clear print set opposite bright racy illustrations. Over a hundred rhymes are included, from old favourites to little-known items such as 'Froggy boggy' or 'Inketty, minketty monketty muddle'. A very approachable collection.

Ring-a-Ring o' Roses by Raymond Briggs (H. Hamilton)
A book generous in the space and illustration given to ten rhymes, so that the reader explores at leisure the soft-coloured pictures, the black and white sketches interspersed with the text, the charming title page. Although Raymond Briggs later won the Kate Greenaway award for his *Mother Goose Treasury* (H. Hamilton) this work has a warmth and unity he failed to achieve in the comprehensive *Treasury*.

Ride a Cock-horse and Other Nursery Rhymes illustrated by Mervyn
  Peake (Chatto & Windus)
Not majority appeal, but the mysterious quality of Mervyn Peake's pictures to these fourteen rhymes is something many teachers will want to share with children. After Peake it is hard to be satisfied with any other interpretation of 'How many miles to Babylon'.

Mother Goose Comes to Cable Street nursery rhymes for today chosen by
  Rosemary Stones and Andrew Mann, illustrated by Dan Jones
  (Kestrel)
Twenty rhymes brought to today's children through settings of city

life. Dan Jones's build-up of detail in the softly-coloured pictures contributes greatly to the interest.

Mother Goose illustrated by Brian Wildsmith (Oxford University
  Press)
Not the best of Wildsmith's work, having little clear sense of commit-ment, but a fairly full collection of the best-known rhymes, with plenty of jolly, coloured pictures.

Workshop comparisons

Hilda Boswell's *Treasury of Nursery Rhymes* (Collins)
Ring o' Roses with drawings by L. Leslie Brooke (Warne)
Humpty Dumpty and Other First Rhymes, illustrated by Betty Youngs
  (Bodley Head)

Games, songs and riddles

Bennett Cerf's Book of Riddles illustrated by Roy McKie (Collins)
One of the most popular of riddle collections, likely to promote lateral thinking. By now the questions (What dog keeps the best time? Why is an egg not like an elephant?) may seem a bit tired to adults, but the simple vocabulary and illustrations are particularly encouraging to inexperienced readers.

Drummer Hoff adapted by Barbara Emberley, illustrated by Ed
  Emberley (Bodley Head)
A chanting cumulative rhyme with explosive climax, illustrated with bright colours over woodcut lines, a technique particularly approp-riate to the toy-soldier solidity of the theme. Awarded the Caldecott Medal.

5 men under 1 umbrella and other riddles by Joseph Low (World's
  Work)
The right-hand page propounds a riddle such as 'Who was the straightest man in England? When is a boy like a pony?', while overleaf are the answers. American in origin but unlikely to cause a problem to young readers on that score.

This Little Puffin . . . compiled by Elizabeth Matterson (Puffin)
Although this collection of finger plays and games was compiled with under-fives in mind, it has proved popular with First School children. A very approachable book, full of enjoyable activities.

This Little Pig went to Market play rhymes for infants and young
  children compiled by Norah Montgomerie (Bodley Head)
A collection drawn from English and Scottish sources, consisting mainly of games of finger play, rocking, foot-tapping, but with some easy singing games included. Margery Gill's black and white drawings provide decoration but not instruction.

Hey Riddle Diddle a book of traditional riddles by Rodney Peppe
  (Kestrel)
Forty-five riddles from old sources presented with sturdy coloured
illustrations, and a necessary page of answers.
Girls and Boys Come Out to Play by Eliazbeth Poston, illustrations by
  William Stobbs (Bodley Head)
One of four volumes making up *The Baby's Song Book*. Each volume
contains about twenty items – some folk songs, some nursery rhyme
settings – with words and piano accompaniment clearly set out, and
enlivened with coloured pictures by William Stobbs.

Workshop comparisons

One, Two, Three, Four number rhymes and finger games compiled by
  Mary Grice with illustrations by Denis Wrigley (Warne)
Finger Rhymes by Dorothy and John Taylor with illustrations by
  Brian Price Thomas and photographs by John Moyes (Ladybird)

Nonsense verse

Selected Cautionary Verses by Hilaire Belloc (Puffin)
It is difficult to select the right age for enjoying Belloc. This paperback selection is useful as an introduction to his work which is now
regarded almost as a classic part of children's literature. A complete
edition is published by Duckworth.
Jabberwocky and Other Poems by Lewis Carroll, pictures by Gerald
  Rose (Faber)
Many people will feel that verses like 'T'was brillig' and 'The Walrus
and the Carpenter' are better in their original version and will find
Rose's illustrations an intrusion, but the book is helpful in gathering
together verses usually scattered. It is arguable that several, especially
the Sylvie and Bruno sequence, are more appropriate to an adult
audience.
Meet my Folks by Ted Hughes, illustrated by George Adamson
  (Puffin)
Twelve humourous, extravagant poems about a highly improbable
family, shot through with Hughes's taste for the macabre.
A Child's Book of Manners by Helen Oxenbury and Fay
  Maschler (Cape)
Cautionary rhymes in a modern style. Don't get mud on the carpet,
disturb the car driver or lose pieces of the jigsaw. All much gentler
than Victorian warnings, with an appeal to sweet reason rather than
demonstration of the ghastly consequences. Enjoyable domestic
detail in Helen Oxenbury's illustrations.

Rhymes without Reason by Mervyn Peake (Methuen)
A handsome edition of verses originally published in 1944. Full-page
colour illustrations, with Peake's usual feeling for the grotesque, face
rhymes slightly reminiscent of Carroll's.
The Complete Nonsense of Edward Lear edited by Holbrook Jackson
(Faber)
The inimitable limericks, verses and songs, with Lear's original
drawings. As a modest introduction one could consider a selection of
lyrics and prose, *A Book of Bosh*, chosen by Brian Alderson, embel-
lished by Lear's drawings, published by Puffin.

Workshop comparisons

Four approaches to illustrating Lear.
The Jumblies and Other Nonsense Verses with drawings by L. Leslie
Brooke (Warne)
The Owl and the Pussy-cat illustrated by Gwen Fulton (Cape)
The Quangle Wangle's Hat pictures by Helen Oxenbury (Puffin)
The Dong with a Luminous Nose and Other Poems pictures by Gerald
Rose (Faber)

Poetry

Major anthologies

Oxford Book of Poetry for Children compiled by Edward Blishen, with
illustrations by Brian Wildsmith (Oxford University Press)
Designed by Blishen to help children make the transition from
nursery rhymes to adult poetry, with content chosen to demonstrate
the many voices and moods of poetry. Wildsmith's bright colour-
work decorates almost every page.
The Faber Book of Nursery Verse edited by Barbara Ireson, illustrated
by George Adamson (Faber)
A bumper book of limericks, rhymes and verse, compiled specifically
for children of First School age. Well-indexed and illustrated with a
slight period flavour by Adamson's black and white sketches.
The Illustrated Treasury of Poetry for Children edited by David Rose
(Collins)
An impressive gathering by an American editor of poetry thoughtful
and merry, written for adults and children. A book to last the whole
lifetime of a family, and containing much that is suitable for Middle
School years and beyond. While the American origin is apparent, the
majority of the entries are by English poets. Illustrations are by
various hands, and generally lack distinction.

Smaller collections

The Puffin Book of Magic Verse chosen and introduced by Charles
 Causley (Puffin)
Spells and curses, ballads and hauntings: a poet's choice which
immediately challenges the conventional school repertoire.
Hi-ran-ho! a picture book of verse compiled by Aidan and Nancy
 Chambers, illustrated by Barbara Swiderska (Kestrel)
Less than fifty poems, but each one given space to make its impact,
and each given individual decorative treatment in black and white or
colour. Not grand poetry, but a very agreeable collection.
A Puffin Quartet of Poets selected by Eleanor Graham, illustrated with
 wood engravings by Diana Bloomfield (Puffin)
A range of emotional and linguistic experience in this selection by a
distinguished editor from the work of major writers of children's
verse: Eleanor Farjeon, James Reeves, E.V. Rieu, Ian Serraillier.
Again, a book which spans the First School years and beyond.

Individual poets

Figgie Hobbin poems for children by Charles Causley (Macmillan)
Figgie Hobbin is a Cornish plum duff which can be eaten as sweet or
savoury: its use here indicates the range of content from sad ballad to
nonsense verse. Evocative line-drawings by Pat Marriott.
Peacock Pie a book of rhymes by Walter de la Mare, with drawings by
 Edward Ardizzone (Faber)
One of the best selections of De la Mare's verse; still fresh and full of
delights, with the bonus of Ardizzone's perfectly-matching drawings.
Now We Are Six by A. A. Milne, illustrated by E. H. Shepard
 (Methuen)
Pooh songs and others, written for Christopher Milne's sixth year.
With time some have become slightly embarrassing, but there is
enough here that is still acceptable to warrant purchase for First
Schools. Shepard's line drawings reinforce the sense of times past.
Hailstones and Halibut Bones adventures in colour by Mary O'Neill,
 illustrated by Leonard Weisgard (World's Work)
Through soft illustrations and poems we explore the world of colour.
'Brown is a freckle/Brown is a mole./Brown is the earth/When you dig
a hole,' Perhaps a bit sentimental for English tastes, but rewarding to
mull over with young children.
A Child's Garden of Verses by Robert Louis Stevenson (Blackie)
Joan Hassall's wood engravings provide a near-perfect setting for
these favourite poems. Alternative illustrators are Eve Garnett, pale
and dreamy (Puffin) or Wildsmith, all bold colour (OUP).

Father Fox's Pennyrhymes by Clyde Watson, illustrated by Wendy
   Watson (Macmillan)
New rhymes in traditional mould, given a New England setting in
light, bright pictures which are rich in detail. An outstanding piece of
book production.

Workshop comparisons

Morning is a Little Child poems by Joan Anglund (Collins)
The Rhyming Rainbow poems selected and illustrated by Cicely Mary
   Barker (Blackie)
My Toys and Other Poems an anthology for infants compiled by Sylvia
   M. Leach (Arnold)
Fives, Sixes and Sevens compiled by Majorie Stephenson with illustra-
   tions by Denis Wrigley (Warne)

Bibliographies

New poetry is included in the annual selection, *Children's Books of the
Year*, published by Julia MacRae in association with the National
Book League. The most valuable list is *Poetry Books for Children*,
published by the Thimble Press, Stroud (Glos), in 1977. For this Alan
Tucker chose over 100 titles and provided generous annotations,
written with perception and enthusiasm. Apart from its use as a
selection tool, the list can form the basis of a poetry workshop,
particularly since all the titles included can be hired as an exhibition
from the National Book League.

3

Interpreting pictures

Contents

The world in pictures   The teacher's task
The artist's aims   References
The child's perspective   Booklist

The world in pictures

Through books we offer children, literally, the world in pictures –
illustrations of everyday life similar to their own, pictures of other
countries and times, excursions into worlds beyond this one, compounded of fantasy and held together by convincing brands of logic.
Children extend their experience through, for example, Kate Greenaway's pictures of fresh neat domesticity, Caldecott's rollicking rural
scenes, the closely observed cityscapes of Charles Keeping and the
mysterious vision of Mervyn Peake. Their view of their own surroundings is confirmed by the simplicity of Dick Bruna or the family
clutter of Shirley Hughes. They play with the enjoyable absurdity of
Galdone's *Three Bears* or Raymond Briggs's *The Elephant and the Bad
Baby*. They gain entry to the miniature world of Beatrix Potter, with
its homely comforts and its sudden terrors.

In a slightly different sense, the world is presented in pictures
through traditional tales from many cultures which are a perennial
source of inspiration to artists. This has been apparent particularly in
the United States, as Elizabeth Gross[1] noted when reviewing winners
of the Caldecott Medal, awarded annually by the American Library
Association for a distinguished picture book. In contrast, England has
for long been famed as the home of fantasy, from Alice onwards, and it
is no accident that many winners of the corresponding British award,

NOTE. Children's books mentioned in this chapter are listed alphabetically by title
after references to academic works.

the Kate Greenaway Medal awarded by the Library Association for distinguished illustration, should have worked in this field. From an early winner, *Mrs Easter and the Storks* (1957), through *Borka* and *Mrs Cockle's Cat*, titles of the 1960s, to the 1978 winner, *Each Peach, Pear, Plum*, the line of the tradition is clear.

In both countries the multi-cultural background of the award winning artists is striking. The mainstream of Anglo-American children's literature has been enriched by figures such as Jan Pienkowski, Victor Ambrus, Nicolas Sidjakov, Feodor Rojankovsky and Marc Simont, who have been able to draw on their links with Continental cultures. The current meeting of many art traditions with a variety of techniques and subject matter has brought to the young a range of visual experience never before available. It has also further complicated the task of selecting stock and has made some critical assessment of the field highly desirable.

Britton and others have reminded us of the great mental leap forward which is made when children grasp that a symbol can represent reality. Usually such observations are associated with letter shapes and words, but they can be applied equally to illustrations. Indeed, children's first understanding that lines and patterns on a page stand for something concrete, which can be touched, smelt, and looked at, comes through pictures. The point when a young child recognizes that the picture in a magazine, on a building block or in a board book represents something he knows is an extremely important one, a landmark in his educational progress. It means that things absent can be recalled and satisfactions relived: the world of books is shown to relate to his world. The delight in the dog next door is reinforced by the book illustration, the flowers in the garden bloom again on the page: his toys are associated and compared with those of the children in the picture book. At this early stage books become a means of strengthening the child's understanding of his own life, and of extending his experience to take in new objects, scenes and lifestyles. One begins with the very simple presentation of individual objects, say through *Indoors*, eight pictures on coloured board, or *Things in the Kitchen*, a modest collection of uncluttered colour photographs. One moves to the portrayal of events and scenes, either at a realistic level, as in the appealing black and white photographs of *Hey, Look at Me*, or with anthropomorphic overtones, as seen in the busy lives of Bear, Rabbit and their friends pictured in the crowded pages of Richard Scarry's *Best Word Book Ever*.

Considering how much time children spend looking at and learning from pictures – in books and in television programmes – it is surprising that so little attention has been paid by educationists to the impact and effect of these visual impressions. A glancing reference to Marshall Macluhan, an acknowledgement of the growing use of audio-visual materials, are almost the extent of the discussion.

A number of research reports on children's viewing habits have, of course, been published, beginning in 1958 with Himmelweit's major work, *Television and the Child*[2]. These have tended to attract more attention from sociologists than from teachers, perhaps because their findings have not been seen as immediately relevant to classroom practice. A basic problem is the lack of a satisfactory method of measuring the effect of viewing on children. Himmelweit concluded: 'the possession of a television set appears to be neither a distinct advantage nor a severe handicap as far as the child's performance at school is concerned.' Her finding is similar to that in a much more recent book, *Children and Television*[3], published in 1976. This summed up: 'We may be groping in the dark when it comes to the effects of the media on adults, but as far as the effects of the media on children are concerned, we may well be lost.'

As with the surveys of children's reactions to picture books, there are few absolutes or precise measures in this subject area. In their absence we edge forward through observation and intuition, which need to be backed by a working experience of a wide range of illustrative material. This chapter seeks to support discussion and individual thinking by looking at picture books from a variety of vantage points, each offering illumination of a cloudy subject.

The artist's aims

We commonly think of 'picture books' as a single category, of appeal to a limited age-range. This is far from the truth. There are books without text – 'pictorial literature' – where the whole message is carried by the pictures; there are books which are designed to help young children identify everyday objects, and others, such as alphabet or number books, which serve as specific learning tools. Sometimes illustrations are a decorative accompaniment to the text, as in much of Errol Le Cain's work. At other times they reinforce what the text says, so that we take in the same points through ear and eye. 'He took his axe and cut the cat open' runs the text of *The Fat Cat* by Jack Kent, 'and out jumped the parson with the crooked staff and the lady with the pink parasol and the seven girls dancing and . . .'. And there we are, counting the girls, looking at the way they dance, making sure the staff is crooked, and finding that the pictures satisfy us on every count. So with *The Elephant and the Bad Baby*, as we check the procession of 'the ice-cream man, and the pork butcher, and the baker, and the snack-bar man, and the grocer, and the lady from the sweet shop, and the barrow boy all running after'.

With each type of book the artist's aims naturally change. Marc Simont[4] has suggested one basic division between illustrations which complement the text, that is, extend it, and those which supplement or repeat it. In the works noted above each artist was bent on the second of these two tasks, an accurate matching of character and incident. To an extent the words are reflected in their pictures. Simont is obviously more interested in the illustrations which extend the text. He feels that the artist's first task is to make himself sympathetic to the basic idea behind the writer's manuscript. 'Once the artist undertakes to illustrate a story, psychologically it becomes his story . . . When the artist makes the story "his own", so to speak, he is free to invent without getting out of character, and thus his pictures will complement – or establish harmony with – the text.' Simont's illustrations to Janice Udry's text in *A Tree is Nice* demonstrate his point.

Selma Lanes makes a division similar to Simont's in her critique of children's literature, *Down the Rabbit Hole*[5]. She chose Arthur Rackham and Maurice Sendak to represent 'the opposite extremes' of picture-making, seeing Rackham as the reporter, honestly recording, breathing 'the indispensable note of actuality into his illustration', and accepting the independent domains of words and pictures. Sendak, on the other hand, conceives of his pictures as 'a kind of background music . . . always in tune with the words', and his concern is to create a psychological atmosphere. To prove her point Lane proceeds to a comparison of Rackham's *The Three Bears* and Sendak's drawings for *Little Bear*.

In practice, Simont's distinction is a nice one. Even when an artist merely 'supplements' a text the result is a personal interpretation, as one can see by comparing two versions of the same tale. Compare, for example, the differing scenes conjured up by Nancy Ekholm Burkett and Svend Otto S. for *Snow White and the Seven Dwarfs*, where we move from mediaeval mystery to a jolly Disney land. Compare also the illustrations for *The Three Bears* by Stobbs and by Galdone. Both artists see the three bears as solid creatures and provide settings of peasant simplicity. However, each adds individual touches. Galdone shows the bears reading in their chairs, with Father Bear reading a tiny book and Baby Bear absorbed in one nearly as big as himself. Stobbs shows Mother Bear adjusting her straw hat and Baby Bear fetching his butterfly net as the family set out on their walk. Even the 'supplementers', in Simont's term, usually do more than repeat the text. We find Stobbs enjoying himself setting a text, 'Time is honey', above Father Bear's bed, and Katrin Brandt in *The Elves and the Shoemaker* finding an unexpected accompaniment to the Brothers Grimm's text, 'What he cut out at night was finished in the morning' – thirty pairs of boots, plus a single one, all laced differently.

Obviously, when author and illustrator are one the two processes, writing and drawing, are brought together more closely and at an earlier stage in the creative cycle. The work of Beatrix Potter is the outstanding example of the balance and interdependence which comes most easily from the author/illustrator, but one can find a similar unity in many more recent makers of picture books such as Ardizzone, Bemelmans, John Burningham and Maurice Sendak.

Features of the current picture book scene are the sophistication of the technology available to artists and publishers, the high level of talent and virtuosity, and the interest in experiment. The richness of visual experience now available in picture books has never been equalled. Consider Wildsmith's sensuous use of colour, Le Cain's delight in ornamentation, the comic genius of Helen Oxenbury, the clarity of Pat Hutchins's pictures. The picture book world has a place for the delicate water colours of Harold Jones and John Burningham, the robust cartoons of Maurice Sendak and Raymond Briggs, the gentle drawings of Shirley Hughes and Arnold Lobel, the peasant art associations of Gerald McDermott and William Stobbs.

Through pen and ink, pastel, gouache, oils and collage, artists present their interpretations of stories and, in the process, their view of life. Behind the finished picture there will have been a history of technical problems faced and solved, and decisions involving the elements of design: colour, texture, space relationships, form and movement. The reader admires the finished result in the formal patterning of Fiona French's baroque decorations to *King Tree*; in the satisfying variations on repeated elements in *Rosie's Walk*, in the strong rhythms of Virginia Lee Burton's *The Little House* or Wanda Gag's *Millions of Cats*; in the controlled composition of Harold Jones in *Lavender's Blue* or of Felix Hoffmann's *The Sleeping Beauty*. The reader responds to the textural interest of *The Toolbox* by Anne Rockwell, the sense of movement in Helen Oxenbury's *The ABC of Things*, the effective use of white space by Ron Brooks in *Aranea: A Story about a Spider*. Book illustration has profited greatly from general moves in the development of the arts, and particularly from the interest in abstract painting, which has had an effect in the treatment of surface, in the use of space, and in new perceptions of colour relationships. One can also find in current work an authenticity rare in the past. See, for example, the meticulously researched settings of Gail Haley, moving from Victorian London in the award-winning *The Post Office Cat* to a Swiss mountain village in *Go Away, Stay Away*, or of Fiona French, recreating African legend in *Aio the Rainmaker*, ancient Egyptian ritual in *Huni* and Dutch interiors in *Hunt the Thimble*.

The artist is, of course, concerned with overall book design and not just the illustrations. The jacket, endpapers, binding, title page, typography and layout are among the parts which combine to make an aesthetic unit. Observe the care given to both general effect and the smallest detail in *Snow White* in the version illustrated by Trina Schart Hyman, or look at the way all elements combine to give aesthetic satisfaction in two versions of the same tale: *Chanticleer and the Fox*, adapted and illustrated by Barbara Cooney, and *The Cock and the Fox*, where Jenny Williams's illustrations support Ruth Manning-Sanders's retelling. The artist will hope that each design aspect will contribute to the effect he wishes to create, signalling mood, genre, period or place. Again the author/illustrator has more freedom for manoeuvre and Virginia Lee Burton[6], who seeks always for an apt juxtaposition of each part, has emphasized the need for perfect correlation: 'Many times I have sacrificed the length of the text or added to it to make it fit the design'.

Apart from this interest in the book as an aesthetic object, and in the technical challenge each new piece poses, illustrators discover a loyalty to their audience and a loyalty to their story. The illustrator is a medium for the revelation of the text. He becomes, in effect, a visual storyteller. Marcia Brown[7], a Caldecott award winner, makes the point vividly. 'Rhythm of speech is echoed in rhythm of line and colour ... The pictures can convey the wonder, terror, peace, mystery, beauty – all he is able to feel or might convey if he were telling the story in words.' Many picture book makers feel this commitment to the text. But many, too, would agree with Roger Duvoisin[8] that the work brings particular artistic satisfactions, with rich opportunity for experiment in colour and design.

Duvoisin suggests that some balance has been achieved, enabling the best picture books to become art creations without losing the particular qualities which give pleasure to children. Sendak[9], on the other hand, once despairingly commented: 'The books have become showcases for artists'. There is certainly a suspicion that some picture books have become too sophisticated, that pictures are pushing text into the background instead of entering into a partnership, that adults too often choose to suit themselves rather than pupils. This issue becomes of immediate importance to the teacher or librarian looking at each season's crop of pictures and trying to select those which have both child appeal and artistic merit. However, for the artist there is no doubt that the picture book world is an exciting one. Beni Montresor[10] spoke for many fellow artists in his Caldecott acceptance speech. 'We have to be open to the marvelous adventure of books made of images ... At this time only one thing should occupy us: To work for images of the highest quality – full, rich, and provocative images that carry the imagination to new heights that will be launching pads for new and always more daring discoveries.'

The child's perspective

Adults are quick to make declarations about children's likes and dislikes, but their reliance in such argument is mainly on observation of small groups or individual children rather than on research findings. It is significant that Virginia Haviland's *Children and Literature*[8], a major guide to reference sources, lists only one study of children's responses to illustration. This is 'Children and their books', a report by two Swedish investigators contained in *The Penrose Annual* for 1962[11]. Their conclusion, after presenting a questionnaire to 300 school children between 7 and 13 years, was that much of the evidence was open to varying interpretation. The points of general agreement include the following:

1 Content matter is regarded as more important than design.
2 Taste in illustration changes with age, young children preferring pictures of familiar objects.
3 Illustrated books are preferred to non-illustrated.
4 Colour is preferred to monochrome.
5 The stronger the colours, the more popular the illustration.
6 The most popular pictures are either totally realistic or totally fantastic.
7 Children under 10 want illustrations with plenty of detail.
8 There seems no awareness of, or response to, artistic merit.
9 Children of 7 years and below like a large type size, at least 12 point. (12 point)
10 Children of 7 years and below like books which are large or small. Other age-groups prefer books of average size.

A study carried out in Berkshire at about the same time came to very similar conclusions. It was devised by Joan Dean, then Primary Schools Adviser for Berkshire, in collaboration with the library service, and was based on the use of a collection of books which were alike in subject matter and age-level but different in size, type of illustration, and layout. Children in six different schools were presented with the collections and asked to make a free choice of the books. Their selection and observations were monitored carefully. As in the Swedish study, the investigation revealed a wide range of response to the same type of illustration, and few areas of agreement. One interesting observation was that choice was often linked with the desire to seem 'grown-up', a factor particularly noted in the middle years of the Infants School. Like the Swedes, the children showed no ability to distinguish between quality and non-quality illustrations.

Celia Berridge, writing in 1980 on 'Illustrators, books and children'[12], surveyed some of the studies in this field. Her conclusion was that, in general, methodology was suspect, and judgments careless. Her article is valuable for its thoughtfulness, and for its list of relevant research reports.

Celia Berridge is currently engaged in doctoral work on children's responses to illustrations, and all indications are that this will be a substantial contribution. In the meantime, research is scanty, and the findings of reported studies are debatable. In such circumstances, teachers and librarians should feel encouraged to undertake their own investigations, observing what children enjoy at different stages, and noting any significant patterns.

They may find that children's approach to pictures changes very much as their approach to books changes, on the lines of the progression outlined in Chapter 1. David Mackay and Joseph Simo[13] have identified a first stage in play in which children discover the properties of objects around them, from which they move to using and playing with the objects. The first picture books are likely to link with this stage, helping with the identification of objects, giving back to the child confirmation of his environment. He sees his games pictured in *Titch*, his memories of the seaside revived by *The Bears who Went to the Seaside*, the world of shopping decisions recalled by *New Blue Shoes*. After coming to some understanding of their surroundings children are ready and eager to play with realistic notions and see how far they can be stretched. This is the time for the visiting elephant dug out of the ground with a teaspoon, in *Balooky Klujypop*, for the surprise discovery of *A Lion in the Meadow*, or belief in the extraordinary friendship of *The Penguin and the Vacuum Cleaner*.

While taste in subject matter changes, there is, as has been noted, little evidence of artistic taste – a point emphasized by Duvoisin[14] when speaking about children's response to pictures. The artist 'can go on making every effort to do tasteful illustrations . . . and he will always be astounded to see what sort of things children may love. For taste, as educated grown-ups know it, is not a children's affair. They do not have good taste or bad taste: they simply are not conscious that there is such a thing.' The most important factor to the children is the story. As Lillian Smith put it in her classic work, *The Unreluctant Years*[15], 'A little child's approach to pictures is first of all a literary one. He expects them to tell him the story he cannot read for himself.' The picture book certainly appeals as a series of visual images, but without the adult analysis of aesthetic pleasure in line, colour and composition. As in any story, the child will look for qualities of warmth, humour and suspense, and characters or situations to which he can relate.

Talking to children, we discover that for them pictures provide a framework on which their imagination can build. Children will go back to favourite illustrations again and again, searching out details, construing and reconstruing meaning. Dorothy Lathrop[16], a Caldecott winner noted for her careful drawings of animals, always felt that children with their fresh vision saw more detail than adults any longer remember to observe. Virginia Lee Burton[17] learnt from experience the sharpness of children's observation, and would put in small details (like the flat tyre of a car on the endpapers of *The Little House*) just to add to their pleasure. She remarked 'With their uninhibited vision, children do not see the world as we do. While we see only what interests us, they see everything.' The child lives among wonders: 'the children's book artist only has to take him by the hand, so to speak, to lead him towards the most imaginative adventures'. Many of us could corroborate from our own experience the strong impression which pictures make on young children. The little boy puts out his hand to stroke the carefully etched squirrel; the little girl takes off her shoes and socks to enter the painted sea. Through pictures children are led into a fresh world in which they move forward to join the action.

The teacher's task

The 'golden rule for teachers' is that 'everything should, as far as possible, be placed before the senses'. So said Comenius in that earliest of picture books, *Orbis Pictus*[18], published in 1659. The sentiments are amazingly modern. Over three hundred years later we find Gladys Williams making a very similar comment in her practical introduction, *Children and their Books*[19]. Through books children are encouraged 'to look, to feel and to listen', three faculties which are 'the means by which we make contact with the world around us'. But the process needs some adult help. Comenius went on to urge the proper presentation and explanation of pictures, which 'implies the use of language so that they will always associate words with objects'. He perceived 'the intimate connection between reality and language'. Again, the modernity is striking, and we can see here proposals in line with Joan Tough's suggested techniques of language development. While Comenius's methods were simple, not to say primitive, they can be regarded as precursors of those advocated by Tough in, for example, Appendix Two, 'Using the pictures', of *Talking and Learning*[20].

The message for teachers is clear. Children need help in looking at pictures. This is apparent if we watch a group of young children given a pile of picture books to look at without any adult guidance. Most leaf through the books quickly, passing from one to another, unable to find the significance of the books without the help of an adult who will discuss what the child sees and help him find a meaning. David Mackay and Joseph Simo emphasize this responsibility in *Help your Child to Read and Write and More*. 'The pictures are no more than a medium through which the child can reach out towards the real world – in the absence of this real world; and it is language shared with an adult which enables this to happen.' While their words were addressed primarily to parents, they are still applicable throughout the First School. We should welcome the opportunity for language development which picture books afford – language development which is fresh and spontaneous within a context of shared enjoyment, far removed from that of so many contrived 'talking together' books. Alan Lynskey in his *Children and Themes*[21] reminds us that this dialogue should arise as naturally as possible. 'It is as simple and as difficult as that; all language is learned in use in response to a situation that calls for it ... The teacher must ensure that children have something to talk about and then take his special place in the sharing process that talking implies, extending the modes of language wherever he can.'

In such discussions it is what pictures mean which will mainly occupy children, not the techniques and methods of the artist. This is to be expected, yet it is a pity that, in a world where visual impressions are so important, the ability to evaluate them is underdeveloped. We have already noted the research finding that children have little aesthetic sensibility, but this may be because they are not helped towards it. Even First School children can become interested in visual effects and techniques, through talk, their own experiments, and direct experience. A prerequisite must be some interest by their teachers in the graphic as well as the descriptive qualities of the books in school. In some professionals dealing with First School children this interest will already be established, but others will feel ignorant and blinkered in the world of visual images.

At present there is little help available to them, and we need to make opportunities to enable such teachers and librarians to educate their visual sense. Review sources are of small assistance; the emphasis in reviewing of picture books is on the stories not the illustration, largely because the reviewers are usually word-orientated people. This is a weakness which review journals should attempt to overcome. Meanwhile, we can seek to increase our understanding of the visual through workshops and study groups with assistance from colleagues or specialists who can help us to see through their eyes. One might begin by looking at a group of books on the same theme – say, the seasons, or starting school – a collection of Greenaway award-winners, or contrasting interpretations of traditional tales, all of which should be available from public library or college resources. Two helpful publications are Bettina Hurlimann's *Picture-book World*[22], much of which is given to a sequence of illustrations grouped by topic, and *Looking at Picture-books*[23]. The latter is the catalogue of a 1973 exhibition arranged at the National Book League by Brian Alderson which set out, ambitiously, 'to consider some of the principles which underlie both the creation of different types of picture book and their critical assessment'. While such lofty aims may not have been realized, both the exhibition itself and the annotated catalogue are noteworthy as almost unique attempts to foster discrimination. They certainly point the way to projects which schools, libraries or Teachers' Centres could organize to encourage comparison and criticism of various pictorial modes.

The kind of picture books available today span all the years of childhood, so throughout the First School and beyond children need help in understanding visual images. Here, as in so many other fields, each school should formulate a policy relating to picture books. Should we buy only books of artistic merit, believing that the school has a responsibility to offer an environment of quality, or should we deliberately buy a range from supermarket shelf-fillers to medal-winners, as part of a programme of encouraging discrimination? Are we content to help children understand the story the pictures tell, or do we want to develop a feeling for the book as a beautiful object? By what programmes can we improve our own judgment? Read Robert Lawson[24] on his fears that children's books will be improved too far, that they will be refined 'to a point where their real vitals become attenuated'. Then read Duvoisin[25] urging the presentation of the well-designed page which 'will also educate the child's taste and his visual sense'. What is our stance on this basic issue? Whatever the policy drawn up, we need to realize that society is becoming increasingly visually orientated. In Beni Montresor's words[26]: 'The idea of the visual book, the book to look at, is an idea of today, and even more, of tomorrow'.

References

1. Gross, E. 'Twenty medal books' in Kingman, L. (Ed) *Newbery and Caldecott Medal Books, 1956–1965* (Boston [Mass], The Horn Book 1965)
2. Himmelweit, H. *and others. Television and the Child* (Oxford University Press 1958)
3. Brown, R. (Ed) *Children and Television* (Collier-Macmillan 1976)
4. Simont, M. Caldecott acceptance speech, in Kingman *op. cit.*[1]
5. Lanes, S. *Down the Rabbit Hole* (New York, Atheneum 1971)
6. Burton, V.L. Caldecott acceptance speech, in Miller, B.M. & Field, E.W. *Caldecott Medal Books, 1938–1957* (Boston [Mass], The Horn Book 1957)
7. Brown, M. Caldecott acceptance speech, in Miller & Field *op. cit.*[6]
8. Duvoisin, R. 'Children's book illustration: the pleasures and problems' in Haviland, V. (Ed) *Children and Literature: Views and Reviews* (Bodley Head 1974)
9. Sendak, M. & Haviland, V. 'Questions to an artist who is also an author', *Quarterly Journal of the Library of Congress*, 28 (Oct 1971), 262–80
10. Montresor, B. Caldecott acceptance speech, in Kingman *op. cit.*[1]
11. Hedvall, A. & Zachrisson, B. 'Children and their books' *The Penrose Annual* (1962) 59–66
12. Berridge, C. 'Illustrators, books and children', *Children's Literature in Education*, 11 (Spring 1980) 21–31
13. Mackay, D. & Simo, J. *Help your Child to Read and Write and More* (Penguin Books 1976)
14. Duvoisin, R. Caldecott acceptance paper in Miller & Field, *op. cit.*[6]
15. Smith, L. *The Unreluctant Years* (Chicago, American Library Association 1953)
16. Lathrop, D. Caldecott acceptance paper in Miller & Field *op. cit.*[6]
17. Burton, V.L. Caldecott acceptance speech *ibid.*
18. Comenius, J.A. *Orbis Pictus* (Facsimile of the English edition of 1659, Oxford University Press 1968)

19. Williams, G. *Children and their Books* (Duckworth 1970)
20. Tough, J. *Talking and Learning* (Ward Lock Educational 1977)
21. Lynskey, A. *Children and Themes* (Oxford University Press 1974)
22. Hurlimann, B. *Picture-book World* (Oxford University Press 1968)
23. Alderson, B. *Looking at Picture-books* (National Book League 1973)
24. Lawson, R. Caldecott acceptance speech in Miller & Field *op. cit.*[6]
25. *op. cit.*[8]
26. *op. cit.*[10]

Booklist

Children's books noted in the text

Although these have been chosen to illustrate particular points, the titles, plus works of other illustrators mentioned, would afford a good introduction to current work. All deserve consideration for First School book collections. For ease of reference they have been arranged in alphabetical order of title.

ABC of Things by Helen Oxenbury (Heinemann)

Aio the Rainmaker by Fiona French (Oxford University Press)

Aranea story by Jenny Wagner, illustrations by Ron Brooks (Kestrel)

Balooky Klujypop story by Ivor Cutler, pictures by Helen Oxenbury (Heinemann)

The Bears who Went to the Seaside by Susanna Gretz (Benn)

The Best Word Book Ever by Richard Scarry (Collins)

Borka by John Burningham (Cape)

Chanticleer and the Fox by Geoffrey Chaucer, adapted and illustrated by Barbara Cooney (Longman)

The Cock and the Fox Chaucer's Nun's Priest's tale retold by Ruth Manning-Sanders, illustrated by Jenny Williams (Angus & Robertson)

Each Peach, Pear, Plum by Janet and Allen Ahlberg (Kestrel)

The Elephant and the Bad Baby by Elfrida Vipont, pictures by Raymond Briggs (H. Hamilton)

The Elves and the Shoemaker the Grimm story illustrated by Katrin Brandt (Oxford University Press)

Fat Cat by Jack Kent (H. Hamilton)

Go Away, Stay Away by Gail Haley (Bodley Head)

Hey, Look at Me by Sandy Grant, photographed by Larry Mulvehill (Kestrel)

Huni by Fiona French (Oxford University Press)

Hunt the Thimble by Fiona French (Oxford University Press)

Indoors by Maureen Roffey (Bodley Head)

King Tree by Fiona French (Oxford University Press)

Lavender's Blue compiled by Kathleen Lines, illustrated by Harold Jones (Oxford University Press)

A Lion in the Meadow by Margaret Mahy, illustrations by Jenny Williams (Dent)

Little Bear by Else Minarik, pictures by Maurice Sendak (World's Work)

The Little House by Virginia Lee Burton (Faber)

Millions of Cats by Wanda Gag (Faber)

Mrs Cockle's Cat by Philippa Pearce, illustrated by Antony Maitland (Constable)

Mrs Easter and the Storks by V.H. Drummond (Faber)

New Blue Shoes by Eve Rice (Bodley Head)

The Penguin and the Vacuum Cleaner by Carolyn Sloan, pictures by Jill McDonald (Kestrel)

The Post Office Cat by Gail Haley (Bodley Head)

Rosie's Walk by Pat Hutchins (Bodley Head)

The Sleeping Beauty by the Grimm Brothers, illustrated by Felix Hoffmann (Oxford University Press)

Snow White and the Seven Dwarfs by the Grimm Brothers, translated by Randall Jarrell; pictures by Nancy Ekholm Burkert (Kestrel)

Snow White and the Seven Dwarfs by the Grimm Brothers, translated by Anne Rogers; illustrated by Svend Otto S (Pelham)

Snow White and the Seven Dwarfs by the Grimm Brothers, translated by Paul Heins; illustrated by Trina Schart Hyman (Heinemann)

Things in the Kitchen by Dean Hay (Collins)

The Three Bears a traditional tale, illustrated by Paul Galdone (World's Work); Arthur Rackham (Heinemann); William Stobbs (Bodley Head)

Titch by Pat Hutchins (Bodley Head)

The Toolbox by Anne Rockwell (H. Hamilton)

A Tree is Nice by Janice Udry, illustrated by Marc Simont (World's Work)

Bibliographies

Booklists go out of date very quickly, and always need supplementing by inspection of new publications. Two modest lists of books for young children (and therefore mainly of picture books) are:

Reading for Enjoyment with 2–5 Year Olds by Elaine Moss (Children's Book Centre, 1975)

Paperbacks for Nursery Schools by Shelagh Webb (National Book League, 1975)

Bettina Hurlimann has chapters on English and American work in her *Picture-book World* (Oxford University Press), which also contains a bio-bibliographical supplement. Gladys Williams, in *Children and their Books* (Duckworth), lists 'Notable (and non-Disneyan) picture-book artists of today'. Jones and Buttrey append a list of 'Picture story books', with a guide to reading and interest age, to their *Children and*

Stories (Blackwell). Peter Hollindale uses a different approach in *Choosing Books for Children* (Elek). Although titles in his book list for the pre-school child have no annotations, they are divided into useful groupings, e.g. Christmas stories, Counting books, Popular series.

Special areas of interest

The lists noted above are general in scope, and of most use in choosing picture story books. The following titles relate to specific areas where the visual image is particularly important.

Books without words

These books immediately present a challenge in interpretation to the reader, who is thrown back entirely on the visual image without the support of text. 'Tell me what the pictures say' is a very usual response but, with a little help, children can be encouraged to translate the pictures into meaning.

A Story to Tell by Dick Bruna (Methuen)
Bruna's use of stylized simple shapes and bold flat patches of colour makes for easy recognition. Here a young child gets up, goes for a walk and finds a companion to share his play. Most of the pictures are instantly comprehensible, but one or two give rise even to adult difference of opinion.

Do you want to be my friend? by Eric Carle (H. Hamilton)
The mouse sets out to find a companion. By clever design the artist keeps us wondering which animal he will try next, and provides small clues to the answer. A book which uses the boundaries of the page as an opportunity, not a restriction, with a great sense of compressed energy and forward movement.

Inter-city by Charles Keeping (Oxford University Press)
A book to demonstrate that books without text are not just for the reception class. Keeping takes us on a train journey in which we observe the changing behaviour of the passengers opposite and the city/suburb/country/city sequence seen through the window. A book occasionally elusive but always stimulating in its appreciation of colour, texture and pattern.

A Boy, a Dog and a Frog by Mercer Mayer (Collins)
Boy and dog set out to catch frog with unexpected consequences. A charming moral tale, one of a series of little books with soft illustrations. Far more incident than in Bruna, but the greater amount of detail and expressive touches make the story easy to follow.

Picture Stories by Rodney Peppé (Kestrel)
Bright cartoons, with each double spread recounting an amusing story. Emphasis on heavy slapstick; easy to understand and good for boosting the fun image of books.

Joe at the Fair by Doreen Roberts (Oxford University Press)
Another book designed as a visual experience with little story-line, as
Joe explores the varied attractions of the fairground. Swirling complex patterns of vivid colours, among which young children may find
object identification difficult. As with Wildsmith's *The Circus*, one
should consider how far direct experience is presupposed and necessary to understanding.
The Great Flood by Peter Spier (World's Work)
Rarely has there been an artist as generous as Peter Spier, master of
the detailed crowd scene. In the story of Noah and the ark's inhabit-
ants he finds a subject perfectly suited to his talents, and executes it
with wit and a variety of page design. Awarded the Caldecott medal.
The Circus by Brian Wildsmith (Oxford University Press)
Not a story, but a series of visual enjoyments, as we are introduced to
the human and animal performers who make up the circus world. The
theme is well suited to Wildsmith's attachment to colour, and here
he uses double spreads to good effect, sometimes matching facing
designs, sometimes carrying the movement confidently across the
double page.

Workshop comparisons

Kipper the Kitten illustrated by Toni Goffe (Macdonald Educational)
Hide-and-seek by Renate Meyer (Bodley Head)
The Sea Voyage by N. Orengo and F. Mello (Black)

Alphabet books

Designed as tools of basic education in past centuries, but now more
likely to be pegs on which the artist can hang a collection of pictures.
In books intended for young children one should check that the letter
forms correspond to those used in teaching reading (eg. ɑ not a; ɡ not
g) and that objects are clearly presented and relate to children's
interests. Books intended for older children can be regarded mainly as
gatherings of pictures and judged accordingly.
b is for bear an alphabet by Dick Bruna (Methuen)
Each double spread has one stylized picture facing one lower case
letter, with check list of words at the end. Some rather unfamiliar
objects: octopus, toadstool, walrus.
ABC by John Burningham (Cape)
Published two years after Wildsmith's alphabet, and borrowing from
his ideas to some extent. Text on coloured paper, objects on white; the
initial letter is given in upper and lower case, while the name of objects
is in lower case only. An uninhibited book, with plenty of movement
in the pictures. Many of the objects (iguana, lion, mouse) coincide
with Wildsmith's choice, and so offer opportunity for an interesting
exercise in comparison.

ABC of Things by Helen Oxenbury (Heinemann)
Helen Oxenbury having fun with the juxtaposition of wasp, weasel
and wolf at a wedding; jam and jelly sent aloft by a juggler. The
introduction of upper and lower case letters comes as a semi-
relevance. The real pleasure is in the soft colours, the impeccable page
design and lettering, and the ridiculous meeting of objects united only
by common initials – witness drooling cat and cow in a chair watching
the approach of crow carrying candle-topped cake.
ABC by Brian Wildsmith (Oxford University Press)
One of the breakthroughs in picture book design, offering dramatic
shapes and colours, enhanced by a background of coloured instead of
white paper. The name of each object is repeated in lower and upper
case. The choice of 'iguana' brought some criticism, but there was
general praise for the cosiness of the kettle, the dignity of the lion.
Wildsmith not only uses colour with relish here but manages to
convey the essential quality of his objects – the watchful nature of the
cat, cumbrousness of the elephant, lugubrious features of the dog.

Workshop comparisons

Anno's Alphabet: an Adventure in Imagination by Mitsumasa Anno
  (Bodley Head)
The Mr Men ABC by Roger Hargreaves (Thurman Publishing)
The Alphabet Book Aa–Zz (Macmillan Education)
A a Apple Rose Isabella Stark's alphabet (Pelham)

Counting books

It is interesting to note the differing approaches to the making of
counting books. Some artists are informed by educational purposes
and try, by repetition and the encouragement of reader participation,
to help children with the basic task of counting from one to ten, or to
move them on to wider number concepts – how many elephants make
a hundred; how many people in a crowd? Occasionally the counting
takes place within the pleasurable context of the cumulative tale.
Many artists, however, are attracted by the comparative freedom of
numbers, as against the alphabet, and take the opportunity to conduct
an exercise in picture making: *Anno's Counting Book* (Bodley Head) is
the obvious example, with its gradual filling of an initially empty
landscape.
Teddybears 1 to 10 by Susanna Gretz (Benn)
Clear pictures, good use of space and easy to distinguish shapes,
linked by a slight story line as the dirty old teddies get a new lease of
life.
Count and See by Tana Hoban (Kestrel)
White numbers on glossy black paper face black and white photographs of objects – many of them things we see every day and yet
hardly notice. A stimulating visual experience.

Numbers by Jan Pienkowski (Heinemann)
One of a series of books on colour, size and shape, rather similar in shape and technique to Bruna's books. Each number is given one double spread; the left hand page gives the number, the name of the object in lower case, and a static picture, while the right hand side carries no text but offers an action picture which invites the reader to check the counting.

The Bears' Counting Book by Robin and Jocelyn Wild (Heinemann)
Counting opportunities set within a story of three naughty bears who find a little house and explore it too vigorously. Eventual repentance and the making of amends.

Workshop comparisons

Ed Emberley's ABC (Dent)
123 and Things by Colin McNaughton (Benn)
Humphrey the Number Horse: a Counting and Tables Book by Rodney Peppé (Methuen)

Play books

There are many signs of a search for ways to combat the inert form of the book – a search which in some cases leads back to the toy books popular in the nineteenth century. Pop-up books are particularly appropriate to family use since their fragility presents problems when subjected to heavy school use. But they have a place in school or public library collections, preferably under supervised conditions to ensure care in handling. Other play books require no special handling, engaging the reader by the use of simple flaps or divided pages, or by involving him in guessing games from the clues provided by the pictures.

Each Peach, Pear, Plum by Janet and Allan Ahlberg (Kestrel)
'Each peach pear plum, I spy Tom Thumb' runs the text, and readers then search the opposite page to find Tom Thumb hidden among the fruit trees. So we are led through the book, with puzzles that tease but rarely defeat. Awarded the Kate Greenaway medal.

The Very Hungry Caterpillar by Eric Carle (H. Hamilton)
The most successful of Eric Carle's attempts to play with the limitations of the printed page. As children follow the holes created by the caterpillar's eating habits, they are also brought to understanding of its transformation to a butterfly, and to a reinforcement of their knowledge of the pattern of weeks and seasons.

The Most Amazing Hide-and-seek Alphabet Book by Robert Crowther (Kestrel)
Simple letter shapes in black card, each hiding an animal made visible through a variety of flaps and tags. Fairly sturdy, but care in use is needed.

Animal Lore and Disorder by James Riddell (Cape)
A tops and tails menagerie, in which cut pages of pictures and text present animals such as the Cophant, the Dachsig, and the Torrse. A challenge to any reader to re-sort them.

Make a Bigger Puddle, Make a Smaller Worm by Marion Walter (Deutsch)
An opportunity for the reader to alter the book's pictures by the use of two mirrors provided in a pocket. A book for 'seeing, changing, imagining . . . and enjoying shapes, patterns and pictures.'

Workshop comparisons

Puss in Boots retold by Christopher Logue from Charles Perrault, four pop-up scenes by Nicola Bayley (Cape)
Ask a Silly Question by Kent Salisbury, illustrated by Joan Allen (Hamlyn)
Peabody's First Case by Ruth Thomson, illustrations by Ken Kirkwood (Dent)

Kate Greenaway Award – Medal Winners 1955–1979

Year	Winner	Title	Publisher
1955	No Award		
1956	Edward Ardizzone	*Tim All Alone*	O.U.P.
1957	Violet H. Drummond	*Mrs Easter and the Storks*	Faber
1958	No award		
1959	William Stobbs	*A Bundle of Ballads* *Kashtanka*	O.U.P.
1960	Gerald Rose	*Old Winkle and the Seagulls*	Faber
1961	Antony Maitland	*Mrs Cockle's Cat*	Constable
1962	Brian Wildsmith	*A.B.C.*	O.U.P.
1963	John Burningham	*Borka*	Cape
1964	C. Walter Hodges	*Shakespeare's Theatre*	O.U.P.
1965	Victor Ambrus	*The Three Poor Tailors*	O.U.P.
1966	Raymong Briggs	*The Mother Goose Treasury*	Hamilton
1967	Charles Keeping	*Charley, Charlotte, and the Golden Canary*	O.U.P.
1968	Pauline Baynes	*A Dictionary of Chivalry*	Longmans Young Books
1969	Helen Oxenbury	*The Quangle Wangle's Hat* *The Dragon of an Ordinary Family*	Heinemann
1970	John Burningham	*Mr Gumpy's Outing*	Cape
1971	Jan Pienkowski	*The Kingdom Under the Sea*	Cape
1972	Krystyna Turska	*The Woodcutter's Duck*	Hamilton
1973	Raymond Briggs	*Father Christmas*	Hamilton
1974	Pat Hutchins	*The Wind Blew*	Bodley Head
1975	Victor Ambrus	*Horse in Battle*	O.U.P.
1976	Gail Haley	*The Post Office Cat*	Bodley Head
1977	Shirely Hughes	*Dogger*	Bodley Head
1978	Janet Ahlberg	*Each Peach, Pear, Plum*	Kestrel
1979	Jan Pienkowski	*The Haunted House*	Heinemann

4

What's in a story?

Contents

Current attitudes   Social values
A literary experience   References
The reader's role   Selection aids
Books to grow on

Current attitudes

What we hope to find in a story depends on our starting point. In the eighteenth and nineteenth centuries 'the story was merely a cloak, at best a thin one, for the moral; its engaging qualities served as means to an end, not as the reason for its existence'.[1] For the literary critic, form – involving plot, style, characterization – is of paramount importance. The child development experts will regard the story as a means of moving the reader forward in his adjustment to society. The reading specialist will look to the story to build up favourable attitudes to reading, to widen vocabulary, and to develop comprehension and fluency. Others will stress the importance of a non-biased approach to issues of class, race and sex, seeing fiction as a means to fostering egalitarian attitudes. However, all groups will take a serious view of the potential of fiction, an attitude which was out of fashion during the first half of this century.

The renewal of interest in children's literature began in the 1960s and took many forms. Some concentrated on the books, others on the readers. Mention has already been made of the influential Dartmouth Seminar of 1966, and of the resulting report, *Growth through English*[2]. This emphasized the personal development consequent on the reading of fiction. The focus was not the material offered, but its effect on the pupil. From such a base it was easy to ignore literary values in a search for 'relevance'. A different stance was taken by those, mainly academics and critics, who sought to establish that children's fiction deserved a place in literary history; that it was, indeed, a part of the general pattern of literature. This school of thought regarded the book solely as a literary object, to be assessed without reference to its potential audience. The case for this purist approach was probably best presented by an article Brian Alderson[3] wrote in 1969, 'The irrelevance of children to the children's book reviewer'.

The Exeter conferences on 'Recent children's literature and its role in education', held annually from 1969–1973, acted as a meeting point for these two views. They helped to establish and propagate literary standards, improved classroom practice, and acted as an all-round stimulus of interest in new and outstanding books. This interest is still carried forward by a lively journal, *Children's Literature in Education*, started by the Exeter Conference team.

Serious consideration of stories for children continues today, but the passage of time has brought new issues to the fore. One is the study of the reader's relationship to the text. What is the stance of the fiction reader? What kind of satisfactions does fiction fulfil? The work of the London Institute of Education, led by James Britton, has been a major influence here. Even as early as 1965 Margaret Meek[4] was putting the reader firmly back in the picture, asserting that critics 'cannot, dare not' ignore the child reader. Choosing for children must include 'an assessment of the kind of satisfaction the books offer children at a given stage in their development'. More recently, the work of Wolfgang Iser has contributed to a reappraisal of the reader's role. In works such as *The Implied Reader*[5] and *The Act of Reading*[6] Iser has helped us realize the creative part played by the reader in the encounter with print.

Some people may regard such theories as academic, in spite of their illumination of practice. Other ideas, however, are founded very firmly in the real world and arise out of perception of social injustice. A range of groups in Britain and America, looking at children's stories, have found in them prejudice, reinforcement of harmful stereotypes, and misleading behaviour patterns. Among these are the Children's Rights Workshop, in this country, and the Council on Interracial Books for Children Inc., which has a New York base.

It is clear that children's fiction is a controversial area in which there is little hope that the arguments will ever be fully resolved. Each professional should be aware of the debating points, and will need to build up an attitude towards them. This chapter will consider stories for the First School in the light of these differing views.

A literary experience

An Edwardian commentator[7] on children's books once observed that 'most children do learn something, consciously or unconsciously, from everything that they read. Their minds are in such a receptive state that the author who writes for children finds himself a teacher whether he likes it or not'. Many of today's authors do, indeed, seem to have a strong teaching instinct, a moralizing streak which may pursue different values from those of the eighteenth and nineteenth centuries but is no less didactic. 'Years ago we threw the old didacticism (dowdy morality) out of the window; it has come back in at the door wearing modern dress (smart values) and we do not even recognise it', wrote John Rowe Townsend[8] in 1967. As both critic and author he was in a good position to perceive trends, but other authors have also been aware of pressure to produce stories as specifics for current ailments. We find, for example, Joan Aiken[9] decrying 'Filboid Studge', stories with 'phoney morality' put in as additional nutriment. She found educationists regarding authors as if 'they were a kind of hot-drink vending machine and you had only to press the right knob to produce an appropriately flavoured bit of nourishment'.

Teachers and librarians must accept some responsibility for such attitudes. How clear are we about literary values; how confident of the worth of a literary experience? The way back to such confidence may be through our adult reading, but, for a renewal of faith in children's literature, several external sources of help exist through, for example, critical journals such as *Signal* and *Children's Literature in Education*[10], or numerous collections of readings – *Only Connect, Children and Literature*, and *The Cool Web*[11].

If we are searching for literary values, one starting point could be consideration of the application of the standard criteria, plot, characterization and style. Although in practice these elements are interwoven and interdependent, it is sometimes helpful to think of them separately and try to decide what makes for quality in each. We may consider the shape of the story-line, its pace, its originality, and find, for example, satisfaction in the neat return to starting situation in *Captain Rocco Rides to Sheffield*[12], the thrust of *The Iron Man*[13], the originality of *The Great Piratical Rumbustification*[14]. Characterization is a major factor in a book's success. When we look back to favourite stories of our own childhood, it is the characters we are likely to call to mind rather than the plot details; it is they who stay and people our imagination, in a sequence running from Mrs Tiggywinkle, Pooh and Toad to Beth, Jim Hawkins and Tom Sawyer. It is usually suggested that characters should be credible, and there is some truth in that. We believe in the hopes and disappointments of Ben, waiting for the present which never came, in *A Dog So Small*[15]. We understand the loneliness of the little girl moved from her old environment in *Charlie, Charlotte and the Golden Canary*[16], and believe in the courage of Ivan in *The Ice Palace*[17], as he strives to rescue his brother. Yet we must not ignore a whole area of fiction where characters need to be stereotypes. The mean Aunt Fidget Wonkham-Strong needs to be worse than anyone's worst aunt to make the point in *How Tom Beat Captain*

Najork and his Hired Sportsmen[18]. In a comedy of situation, like *Maggy Scraggle Loves the Beautiful Ice-cream Man*[19], or even *My Naughty Little Sister*[20], too much subtlety holds up the action, and characters need to be sketched in brief outline. There are stories which require flat characters and those which require three-dimensional characters, and we need to establish the difference before trying to judge the author's success.

Literature, said the Bullock Report[21], 'brings the child into an encounter with language in its most complex and varied forms', a statement rightly emphasizing the engagement with words which is at the heart of the literary experience. It is style which, ultimately, decides the quality of a story, for, without a facility with words, the author cannot unfold the plot or portray the characters in a way which commands interest. Style may be enjoyed by children without being identified by them – the rhythmical text of Sendak's *Where the Wild Things Are*[22] illustrates the point – but it is essential that we, the adult selectors of books for children, should train ourselves to be sensitive to the words which carry the story. There are no absolutes; our response to language is very much one of personal taste, but we can begin to find touchstones by listening to the individual voice of each writer, and by clarifying our ideas through discussion with others. What, for example, is our view of the following extracts?

a) 'It was a magical morning with a silence like all the secrets in the world, and a light like happiness. As the boys ran down the slope towards the sea the stones skidded and clattered under their feet, making a great noise in the quiet morning.'[23]

b) 'While the others were out walking, Dad came home again. He left the truck outside the house. He gave it a little wash and a rub before going in. He put the polishing cloth under the seat in the driver's cab. On the back of the seat he had stuck pictures of all the children and Mum. He always felt like having them with him when he was out driving. If he met anyone he liked very much he would take the whole seat out of the lorry and show them the nice pictures.'[24]

c) 'The little man had a brown suit with black buttons, and a brown tie and shiny shoes – all most respectable and handsome. He worked in a neat office and wrote down rows of figures in books, and ruled lines under them. And before he spoke, he always coughed *"Hrrrrm!"*.'[25]

d) 'Christmas had been a mad and merry time in the Lyntons' house. All the children had come home from school in high spirits, looking forward to plenty of good food, presents and jollifications.'[25]

e) 'Peter felt about with his toes under a large rock. He could feel the ridges in the rock and some seaweed that seemed to flutter when he touched it. But he couldn't discover the ridgy shells he was probing for. The bottom of Richard's feet only just reached the surface of the water. He was patting it with his feet, making ripples and turning the water cloudy.'[27]

Jones and Mulford[28] have pointed out that among the multiplicity of satisfactions which stories offer, enjoyment of form is patently one. We should, therefore, be looking for ways in which to develop children's sense of form – encouraging them to anticipate the possible course of events in a story, understanding where the climax of the action occurs, forming an opinion on the final resolution. What kind of story do they expect, for example, from the opening of *Meal One*[29]? Was the boy dreaming all those adventures? Is the ending an anticlimax? Could the children suggest an alternative ending? *It's Too Frightening For Me*[30], says the title page of one of Shirley Hughes's stories. The first page describes the big deserted house. 'Nobody went in and nobody came out, except for a big tom cat, as black as a shadow'. The next page shows the two brothers daring one another to squeeze through the gate. What's going to happen? Are we disappointed at the lack of ghosts? Are there some parts which are hard to believe? Could we do better? In order to make these kind of predictions or judgments the child has to understand the value systems operating in the narrative. Humorous books often present difficulties in this way. Consider, for example, what a child needs to know to understand the sequence in Benchley's *The Magic Sledge*[31] in which the bear decides to eat at least one of the other passengers and an argument ensues. 'Then you can't eat me. It would be like eating your insurance policy'. 'You're not a policeman's horse. You're a lawyer's horse', etc.

Assessing stories in terms of plot, characterization and style is an interesting discipline, but at some stage we have to put back the separate components and look at the story as a whole. C. S. Lewis[32] was among literary commentators who have seen the danger of concentration on specific aspects; in so doing one may overlook the real raison d'être of the narrative, its theme. 'The author's plot is only a net of time and event for catching what is not really a process at all.' It is the 'internal tension at the heart of every story, between the theme and the plot' which constitutes its chief resemblance to life. Before leaving the standard criteria, however, it may be helpful to record some variations suggested by Sidney Robbins in discussion. The questions he addressed himself to answering were:

'Is the book linguistically alive? Is the language individual, lively, sensitive? Is the story imaginatively and humanly worthwhile? Will it draw children into its spell?'

The consistency of advice from those who see stories primarily as a literary experience is remarkable. Literature is an experience, not a resource; we should think of it as 'being', not as 'being for' some other purpose. If we need convincing, have forgotten or overlooked the power of story, the best first course may be not an intellectual approach through analysis of what makes a good narrative, but a dose of some outstanding current work, to remind ourselves of the satisfactions literature can afford. And once we have renewed our own belief in the power of story, we shall look for ways of opening up these pleasures to children. One of the most effective methods, storytelling, is considered in Chapter 9, and other suggestions can be found in Chapter 8, 'Encouragements to reading'.

The reader's role

We can see that stories have fascinated man for centuries. Still part of our current repertoire are the legends of the Greek gods, the exploits of the Trojan warriors and the wandering Odysseus, Aesop's fables, the mediaeval romances of King Arthur, and the tales of Chaucer's pilgrims. Man has an insatiable appetite for stories, whether relayed in print, on radio, through television or street corner gossip. 'Nature, not art, makes us all storytellers', observed Barbara Hardy[33]. 'We narrate to each other and ourselves . . . We live in narrative phantasmagorias as we live in countries and climates.' But just what is the stance of the reader or listener to these fictions is by no means clear.

For many years it was assumed that the reader took on the personality of one or more of the storybook characters, and found emotional release in this vicarious experience. Whitehead in *Children's Reading Interests*[34] noted that many earlier studies of children's reading preferences showed that a major motivation was the desire 'to obtain vicarious imaginative satisfaction of a wish fulfilment kind'. The returns from his own research contained many titles where 'it seems reasonable to suppose' the reader's satisfaction was achieved 'by identification with a hero or heroine into whose shoes the reader steps for the time being in order to enjoy at second hand an emotionally gratifying sequence of adventures, dangers and triumphs'. A similar belief was one of the driving forces behind Leila Berg's determination to provide stories which reflected the lives of urban children and so enabled them 'to have their personal identity confirmed'[35] – a project which resulted in the Nipper series published by Macmillan from 1968.

A completely opposite view was propounded by D. W. Harding in a 1962 article for the *British Journal of Aesthetics*[36], in which he concluded that the fiction reader, in actuality, adopts an onlooker or spectator role, in which he is outside the events, not participating in them. Harding also criticized the loose use of the term 'identification' for a series of processes which included 'empathy, imitation, admiration or recognition of similarities'. It is this view of the reader as spectator which has been developed and proselytized by the London Institute of Education staff over the last few years. The great publicity given to D. W. Harding's thoughts has certainly reduced the blanket use of the psychological term 'identification', but the arguments advanced have not been entirely persuasive. In the third edition of

Growth through English, published in 1975, John Dixon, commenting on developments since the 1966 Dartmouth seminar, found that 'the implicit emphasis on the spectator role has tended to narrow the definition of literature'. It may be that we phase in and out of the participant role; that we develop special sympathy or rapport not with one character but with a range, depending on the way the events of the story relate to our own circumstances or disposition.

The London Institute team has helped to further understanding of stories in another direction, through discussion of their function as templates of the child's (or adult's) own storymaking, and by directing attention to the process of 'getting into' a story. If, as Tolkien[37] has suggested, the author creates a 'secondary world' which he invites the reader to enter, then we need to consider how the reader is helped into that world and how his belief in it is maintained. The inexperienced reader needs the terms of reference established at a very early stage, while a sign of a mature reader is his willingness to wait, even though mystified, until a setting unfolds. Almost any selection of books will demonstrate a range of techniques used by the author to encourage the reader over the threshold, as the following examples, chosen at random, show.

My Naughty Little Sister Goes Fishing by Dorothy Edwards (Methuen)

The author is at pains to establish relationships and time sequence: 'A long time ago, when I was a little girl, I had a sister who was very much younger than me'. She also guides the audience to an appropriate reaction: 'most of the naughty things she did were so funny that no one was cross with her for very long . . .'

The Land of Green Ginger, by Noel Langley (Kestrel)

The Forest of Boland Light Railway by Denys Watkins-Pitchford (Hodder)

Both writers acknowledge the presence of the reader, but in very different terms. Noel Langley chooses an elaborate style, reminiscent of Arabian fantasy. 'May fortune preserve you, Gentle Reader. May your days be filled with constant joys, and may my story please you, for it has no other purpose. And now, if you are ready to begin, I bring you a tale of heroes and villains . . .'

The initial purpose of 'B.B.' (ie Denys Watkins-Pitchford) is to make us see his setting. 'The Forest of Boland, where the gnomes in this story lived, was huge. It would have taken you three days and a bit to walk from one side to the other.'

The Tale of Mrs Tiggy-Winkle by Beatrix Potter (Warne)

The Weathermonger by Peter Dickinson (Gollancz)

Author and reader are outside the story, observing its events. Beatrix Potter used a simple, conventional beginning: 'Once upon a time there was little girl called Lucie, who lived at a farm called Little-town'. Peter Dickinson, writing for children above First School age, forces the reader's close attention to the small clues which eventually enable a picture to emerge. Although the narrative is not in the first person, we are privy to the sensations and thoughts of the main character. 'He woke up suddenly, as if from a deep sleep full of unrecoverable dreams. He was very uncomfortable. The light was too bright, even through closed eyes, and there was something sharp and hard jutting into one of his shoulder-blades.'

As we read the stories children make up, or watch their play and drama, we can frequently see an association between the stories read to the children and those they create. Margaret Spencer (née Meek) provides several examples in a chapter for *Children Using Language,* while the Rosens in *The Language of Primary School Children*[38] link stories read, stories day-dreamed and stories written, and call the activity 'storying'. Their view was that 'for young children, certainly, receiving, retelling and composing stories can be seen as different parts of the same process.' If we accept this view, our concept of the reader's role immediately widens, and our responsibility for introducing models of richness and quality increases. The Rosens are quite clear that 'a diet of thin recipe stories is not the best help to the story-teller' and urge that teachers should be aware of our great cultural heritage of stories and open it to children.

The greatest insights into the role of the fiction reader in the last few years have come from the writings of Iser[39], whose closely reasoned works are hard to summarize. From him we have built up a view of the reader as someone actively engaged with text, and we have realized that for each individual, or at each re-reading, the text changes. The impact of a story comes from the way the reader's imagination works on 'the gaps in the text'; as the reader shades in the outline of given situations these take on a reality of their own. Success depends on the extent a text 'can activate the individual reader's faculties of perceiving and processing'. Iser's books are concerned with adult literature, but even such a simple book as *Rosie's Walk*[40] provides an illustration of his thesis, in its deliberate provision of space in which the imagination of the reader can make its contribution.

Books to grow on

It is the idea that stories in some way promote personal growth which has inspired English teaching over the last few decades, as the Bullock Report recognized. Literature 'confronts the reader with problems similar to his own, and does it at the safety of one remove', so providing reassurance and even resolution of personal difficulties. It also offers an entrée into the thoughts and experiences of people of other times or countries, or with life-styles different from the reader's, and in this way it enriches the imagination and increases understanding. The link between literature and children's developmental needs has been touched on in Chapter 1, and many adults can testify to this association from their own early reading or their current contacts with children.

There can, however, be a point at which we move from choosing books which reflect children's interests, to selecting stories to cure particular ills, and at that point we are in danger of selecting not because a book has intrinsic merit but because a book's theme matches our checklist of problems. This is a limiting attitude, limiting our view of the function of literature, and limiting our view of the reader's response. It ignores the role of fantasy, it overlooks the impact of story at a symbolic or emotional level. 'Works of the imagination carry the mind out of self', said Coleridge. Too often book selection policies merely imprison the mind within a domestic context of triviality. Here again we are back to a basic issue which requires staff discussion. The books noted below indicate some of the interests currently being pursued in children's fiction. While all are recommended for First School stock, they may also be used in workshops on selection policy.

Mirror images

The young child's effort to understand his environment is part of a struggle which continues throughout life. We are motivated from our earliest years, as Ann Durell[41] recently put it, by 'a central fantasy of a controllable environment', and one of the great satisfactions of literature is its support of this fantasy by superimposing shape and pattern to events. We like the happy ending with the family reunited, the pioneers establishing a new home, hard work or suffering justified. This satisfaction can operate in some of the simplest stories as well as the most complex.

A linked need is that of establishing one's identity, and the young child, with his strong egocentricity, has this as a basic concern. 'Where did I come from, to whom do I belong, are other children like this?' are fundamental questions which are answered by unpretentious stories showing other children operating in the familiar world of morning and bedtime routines, passing seasons, birthdays and outings. These mirrors of the world the child already knows offer a new perspective on his life and a realization that many experiences are widely shared. All these new understandings are like pieces in a mosaic which help the child build a self-image, and move him forward to the next stage in development, the concept of sharing. It is the self-image which guides the child's behaviour, giving some confidence in new situations, and helps offset his inevitable feelings of helplessness. Piaget[42] was very conscious of the child's role as agent of his own growth, first through assimilation, that is the absorbing and organizing of experience, and then through accommodation, a modifying process which steers the child into adaptation to the world around. Stories will be among the influences helping this growth, and those listed below illustrate some approaches to this presentation of the everyday. When selecting titles, we should look for warmth in the relationships in addition to characters and situations which are easily recognizable. We should also seek to offer a range of settings so that each child, whatever his family background, can find some lines of association.

Home

The Baby by John Burningham (Cape)
One of John Burningham's 'Little Books' with domestic and school settings. Each left-hand page has a brief sentence and faces an uncluttered picture in soft colours. The text has a slight therapeutic element.

My Teddy Bear by Chiyoko Nakatani (Bodley Head)
More detail and colour than Burningham uses, but still a clear, simple line. The book presents the daily round of a pre-school child, offering patterns for comparison. Teddy shares meals and walks, is given a bath, and finally settles down for the night.

Time to Go by Hilary Wills (Methuen)
The clock moves on relentlessly from eight o'clock, getting up time, to nine, when Granny's train arrives. Argued over by adults – home untidy, father ineffective – and generally approved by children for its comic crises. A book to compare with Shirley Hughes's *Tom and Lucy's Day* (Bodley Head), a cosier documentation of the domestic round, and Felicity Sen's *My Family* (Bodley Head), a child's eye view of a one-parent family.

Thomas Tidies his Room by Gunilla Wolde (Hodder)
An appealing, sturdy central character tidies up and finds a lost toy in the process. One of a series of stories of Scandinavian origin showing Emma and Thomas unimpeded by sexual stereotypes, e.g. in *Emma's Workshop*, or *Thomas Bakes a Cake*, which lose as story as the didactic element grows.

School

My Brother Sean by Petronella Breinburg, illustrated by Errol Lloyd (Bodley Head)
Almost a classic story of a little boy's first day at school, with trauma moving into a kind of reconciliation. A book defended and attacked with equal fervour by adults: 'it's too upsetting'; 'it's not grammatical'; 'it vividly portrays a black child's experiences.' Dorothy Butler

provides a child's verdict in *Cushla and her Books* (Hodder). 'Cushla solicitously kissed his howling little face at every reading . . . Her identification with Sean was complete.'

Willy Bear by Mildred Kantrowitz, illustrated by Nancy Winslow Parker (Bodley Head)
An interesting sequence in which the boy transfers his fear of going to school to his bear, and in comforting Willy finds courage to set a good example. Psychological truth, but the dialogue may be uncomfortably sentimental for English adults. The clear stylized pictures open up plenty of opportunities for talk.

My Nursery School by Harlow Rockwell (H. Hamilton)
Father delivers, Mother collects, and in between there is the long day of school for the child to enjoy or endure. A documentary account with very clear illustrations.

I went to School one Morning by Guido Waldman, illustrated by Michael Charlton (Bodley Head)
The procession to school through town streets of a five-year-old and Mother. Cosy family relationships.

Friends

Ian the Referee by Allan Ahlberg, pictures by Janet Ahlberg (Collins)
Homely cartoon-style pictures with town settings for Sam's attempt to keep five children and a dog occupied. All, amazingly, is calm by the time the parents arrive home.

Dogger by Shirley Hughes (Bodley Head)
Plenty of detail in the illustrations to a familiar tragedy – the loss of a favourite toy – with help coming from an unexpected quarter. Awarded the Kate Greenaway medal.

Nini at Carnival by Errol Lloyd (Bodley Head)
Errol Lloyd's Jamaican associations are reflected in this touching tale of Carnival time. But who helped Nini become Queen of the Carnival? Was it a fairy godmother or her kind friend Betti?

Spud comes to Play by Joan Solomon, photographs by Richard Harvey (H. Hamilton)
One of an attractive series designed to show 'children of today living together in a multi-racial community.' Lively colour photographs, short text and simple sentence structures. Not tied closely to any age-group.

Interest in stories of family and school is maintained throughout the First School years. One can move through a sequence from Gazelle books – 50 page complete stories intended for inexperienced readers – such as Denise Hill's *No Friends for Simon* or Godfrey Young's *The Short Cut* (H. Hamilton), though spirited adventures such as Astrid Lindgren's *Six Bullerby Children* (Methuen) to gems like Philippa

Pearce's gently humorous short stories, *What the Neighbours Did* (Longman) or her distinctive treatment of a familiar family problem *The Battle of Bubble and Squeak* (Deutsch).

Counsellor's corner

The problems of children may seem small compared with those of adults, but in some way their pains are sharper. Adults have a clearer appreciation of the transience of life, while children are caught in the trap of an unmoving present. They are aware of problems without resolution – loneliness, fears, jealousy – and sin without redemption – tempers, aggression, cheating. We are unlikely to find a computer-match approach successful: one child's fears are another one's fun; a book which clears up one difficulty may stir up another discontent. Bibliotherapy works through an engagement with the reader's emotional concerns, and it is not possible to forecast how and when that connection will be made.

Nevertheless, it is reassuring for children to realize that other children have troubles. Fiction is a valuable agent here, channelling strong emotions and suggesting ways of handling them. It is also a source of vicarious experience, as through it we meet death, separation, heroism, and adjust our view of life accordingly. Such encounters need tactful management. It is wrong to make children grow up too quickly, arrogant to pretend an exact knowledge of their problems, and mistaken to see fiction as a panacea.

Even the weak . . .

Tony's Hard Work Day by Alan Arkin, pictures by James Stevenson
    (Deutsch)
There was plenty of work to do when the family moved into the country, but nobody wanted Tony's help. So he set out on a project of his own, building a fantasy house even better than the real one. Satisfying partly because of the built-in ambivalence.
Titch by Pat Hutchins (Bodley Head)
Pete has a great big bike, Mary has a big bike, and Titch has only a little tricycle. But one day he gets ahead of the group. Consoling story with bright, jolly pictures.
David's Witch Doctor by Margaret Mahy, illustrated by Jim
    Russell (Franklin Watts)
Big and little ones get attention; middle ones get nothing. When he realized this, David set out to get help from the strange doctor over the road, and he found it in a very practical form. Credible resolution and good characterization.

Big Boss by Anne Rockwell (World's Work)
Small frog defeats hungry tiger and scheming fox in a series of
amusing episodes. Easy-to-read text and amusing pictures.

Extended family

The Gorilla Did It by Barbara Hazen, illustrated by Ray Cruz
  (Blackie)
The old theme of transference of blame explored with humour and
warmth. The bad gorilla made the bedtime rumpus, but he's sorry
and really means to be good. Meantime a late-night cookie settles him
down. Reminiscent of the emotions worked out with such brilliance in
Sendak's *Where the Wild Things Are* (Bodley Head).
A Baby Sister for Frances by Russell Hoban, pictures by Lillian
  Hoban (Faber)
'Things are not very good here any more', says Frances, as the new
baby's needs overshadow hers. By the end of this tender little story
she realized that 'A family is *everybody all together*'. One of a series of
witty but gentle moral tales about Frances and her family.
Peter's Chair by Ezra Jack Keats (Bodley Head)
The jealousy of the new baby explodes when Father wants to paint
Peter's little chair pink, but parents and Peter reach out to achieve a
reconciliation and new attitudes.
Noisy Nora by Rosemary Wells (Collins)
Middle-child Norah is continually making a noise to call attention to
her wants. It's strange what a greater effect silence has. A warm-
hearted story in verse, accompanied by soft drawings of the Mouse
ménage.

Fears and fury

High Climb by John Escott (H. Hamilton)
One of the Antelope series of 80 page stories intended for six to
nine-year-olds. Neil can't face the challenge of the gang and runs away
from school rather than climb the old poplar tree. As a result he finds
new friends and unexpected courage. Agreeable cast of children and
adults.
Boy, Was I Mad by Kathryn Hitte, pictures by Mercer Mayer
  (Collins)
The boy dashes out of the house in a fury, intent on running away. It's
such a nuisance that he has so many interesting encounters that he
absentmindedly gets back home at the end of the day, tired out and
content. Contrast with the approach of *The I Was so Mad I could have
Split book* by Gisela Frisen and Per Ekholm (Black) on which adult
opinion sharply divides: 'Wonderful therapy', 'Mother ridiculously
subservient' etc.

Mr and Mrs Pig's Evening Out by Mary Rayner (Macmillan)
A pity that short-sighted Mrs Pig didn't realize that the evening
sitter-in was the Wolf. A boisterous comic fantasy in which the little
pigs foil Mrs Wolf's supper plans. Catherine Storr has also used the
wolf as fear-symbol to good effect in *Clever Polly and the Stupid Wolf*
(Faber).
Lucy Runs Away by Catherine Storr (Bodley Head)
A desire to prove that the youngest of the family can look after herself
drives Lucy to run away to find adventure – and that is exactly what
'the mysterious outlaw on his coal-black horse' does meet. Very good
adult/child relationships, and an engaging heroine.

Pushing out the boundaries

Once children have a grasp of reality they begin to want to test its
limits and properties. 'What would happen if . . . ? What's the biggest
possible . . . ? Supposing you could reach as far as . . . ?' The jokes,
the puns, the tall tales, are in a way a reinforcement of children's
understanding of real life. They are also a means of cultivating the
imagination, on whose exercise much of our response to people and
situations depends. On a symbolic level the excursions into fantasy
can bring us back to reality with a deeper appreciation of its qualities
and potential – as the history of allegory shows. 'Fantasy is both the
necessary preparation for action and the means of delaying it', as
I. Leng noted in his survey, *Children in the Library*[43].

If we look at children's writing, we see that the division between
fantasy and reality is extremely thin; one flows into the other as if
children were unaware of any distinction. It is also significant that
young children accept without question stories about talking animals,
as a natural progression from their feeling that their toys are real
friends. The animal characters serve to distance problems or to make
them more acceptable. However amazing the story, it needs a very
careful groundwork of reality in order to capture our belief and enable
us to accept the strange events which follow. If we consider outstanding fantasies such as *Wind in the Willows*, *The Borrowers*, the *Moomin*
stories of Tove Jansson, or the *Narnia* sequence of C.S. Lewis, we can
see that it is the building up of small realistic detail which assists the
'willing suspension of disbelief' and entry into a magical world.

Home-based

Horse-on-Wheels by Ruth Ainsworth (H. Hamilton)
Undemanding story in the Gazelle series of the younger brother whose
attachment to his wooden horse blossoms at night, when they slip off
to meet the other animals in Farmer Jones' paddock. Lucky Tom, but
then, as the animals agree, he was 'nice enough to be a foal and not a

boy at all'. Understanding family background.

Kate and Sam Go Out by Michael and Joanne Cole (Methuen)
An amusing imaginative exercise, as the children decide how to get to Grandma's house. By horse, balloon, crane? In the event they walk round the corner and arrive in time for tea.

There's No Such Thing as a Dragon by Jack Kent (Abelard)
Light-hearted fancy with a moral. The more the dragon was ignored, the larger it grew. When it was accepted as one of the family, it went back to being a convenient pet-sized dragon. Why all the bother? 'I think it just wanted to be noticed,' said Billy.

What's Inside the Box by Ethel and Leonard Kessler (World's Work)
The great big box wasn't there yesterday, and the animals gather round to guess what is inside. Clearly a monster, as they discover four legs, twenty toes and two heads. A fun guessing game, in which the reader reaches the answer first.

Mr Bear's Meal by Chizuko Kuratomi, illustrated by Kozo Kakimoto (Macdonald & Janes)
One of a series about a good-natured but naïve bear who is always getting into trouble for the best of motives. His adventures in the Rabbits' kingdom are just saved from disaster by each side managing to see the other's viewpoint. Inside the fun, a gentle lesson in charity.

One step out

The Castle of Yew by Lucy Boston (Bodley Head)
A book foreshadowing the deeper mysteries of Lucy Boston's Green Knowe series, and an object lesson in moving from reality to fantasy, as Joseph explores the magic garden and gains entry to the Castle and its dangers.

Nurse Matilda by Christianna Brand, illustrated by Edward Ardizzone (Hodder)
Satisfying wish-fulfilment story, as we witness the reformation of the 'terribly, terribly naughty' Browns, and the transformation of stern, ugly Nurse Matilda, growing in loveliness with the children's growth in virtue.

The Piemakers by Helen Cresswell (Faber)
Tall tale of the great pie-making competition of Danby Dale, when skulduggery is defeated and fortitude rewarded. Some of Helen Cresswell's best work, each word exact, each character an individual creation.

The Great Jelly of London by Paul Jennings, pictures by Gerald Rose (Faber)
A plan worked out in such detail that we must believe in it. Paul Jennings has fun with a philanthropic scheme which involves buying the Albert Hall and filling it with jelly, and the counter-plots of wicked Sir William Grugsby and accomplice Diabolical Len Bodge.

The plot complexity and background sophistication require a mature readership.

The Great Millionaire Kidnap by Margaret Mahy, pictures by
  Jan Brychta (Dent)
The expected turned on its head, as the victim plans an even bolder plot with his captors, Hardly Likely and Scarcely Likely. A rich, racy story with great words like 'tintinnabulation' to relish, and a surprise role for Pretty Likely.

Convention overturned

Burglar Bill by Janet and Allan Ahlberg (Heinemann)
Every night Burglar Bill gets out of his stolen bed, has some stolen supper, and goes off to his work, stealing things. The absurdities played to the full in visual and verbal jokes, and a necessary repentance at the end.

Wildcat Wendy and the Peekaboo Kid by Nancy Chambers
  (H. Hamilton)
A Gazelle book with all the ingredients to pull in an audience: a Wild West setting, heroine in the Pippi Longstocking tradition, faithful, sagacious horse, bully to overcome, and toasted marshmallows to keep up strength. For a more detailed reworking of the Western theme try Alan Coren's action-packed saga of the seven-year-old sleuth, *The Lone Arthur* (Robson Books).

The Flying Postman by V.H. Drummond (Faber)
Text and pictures in perfect accord in this award-winning story of the helicopter postal service that over-reached itself. Very satisfying story line – adventure, disaster, recovery.

Sailor Jack and the 20 Orphans by Margaret Mahy, pictures by
  Robert Bartelt (Puffin)
A failed pirate, Miss Emily Jones of the famous submarine family of Davy Jones, and a sailor crew of monkeys get together with twenty orphan boys on a floating island for a life-long voyage of enchantment. A witty text points up the improbabilities.

Green Smoke by Rosemary Manning (Longman)
Tales within a tale, with R. Dragon, 1,500 years old and addicted to almond buns, telling Susan stories of Cornish giants and heroes. In a tradition stemming from Kenneth Grahame's *The Reluctant Dragon* (Bodley) and continued in Rosemary Weir's *Albert the Dragon* (Abelard).

Imaginative free-wheeling

There is a perceptible difference, hard to define, between the little forays into the world of fantasy, with careful return to base, described above, and those stories which exist in a self-made world. The distinction is similar to that small move from comic to nonsense verse. The orthodox fantasy builds up, brick by brick, the façade of the world we know, and then springs the surprises. Just a few books attempt a surrealist approach, making their point by ignoring rather than extending natural laws. Some may be shaped by basic wish-fulfilment themes, power, food, sex, while others are an expression of a zest for life and adventuring. Casting off with them, free of the everyday, can be an invigorating experience, reaching down to the springs of the child's own creativity.

Animals Should Definitely Not Wear Clothing by Judi Barrett,
   drawn by Ron Barrett (Kaye & Ward)
Pages of various colours carry the brief text in bold print, while facing pages present the grotesque consequences of issuing clothing to a group of animal friends. Less a story than a series of imaginative exercises which, if extended, might become boring, but here keep interest by the wit and inventiveness of author and illustrator. Some similarity in form with John Burningham's *Would You Rather...* (Cape), a series of dilemmas with no obvious answers. Would you rather be crushed by a snake, swallowed by a fish, eaten by a crocodile or sat on by a rhinoceros? Would you rather be lost in the fog, at sea or in a crowd?

Come Away from the Water, Shirley by John Burningham (Cape)
A winner for children old enough to perceive the generation gap. Sedate parents on left-hand pages issue instructions to their daughter, while she, on right-hand pages, engages in a dangerous meeting with pirates.

Timothy's Dream Book by Pierre Le-Tan (Macmillan)
In the bedtime story Little Rabbit wanted to be a postman. Timothy dreams up more interesting careers for himself, caretaker to the moon, assistant to tired statues, or the first nose explorer in the world. A challenge to add to his list.

The Long Slide by Mr and Mrs Smith (Cape)
No lead in, no explanations: the reader is confronted with a picture of downland, three strange toys, and a slanting red line at one side. That great luxury, an adventure without explanations.

The Hat by Tomi Ungerer (Bodley Head)
The black top hat with magenta sash lands at the feet of Benito Badoglio, a penniless one-legged veteran, and proceeds to transform his life. One incredible adventure follows another, narrated and drawn with an extravagance and panache typical of Ungerer.

Other life styles

The Bullock Report noted the value of stories in presenting 'the thoughts, experiences and feelings of people who exist outside and beyond the reader's daily awareness.' It is when children have the security which comes from understanding their own environment that they are ready to venture further to fresh encounters. At this stage they can begin to read tales set in the past or in distant countries, meet situations far beyond those of the domestic round. The stories' characters and events become part of an accumulating knowledge of people and situations built up by direct and indirect experience.

At the point when children become impatient with the cosy scenes of their early books they need stories, as Jones and Mulford stressed, 'as an earnest of growing up, because through them they transcend the limitations of their state'. Germane to the process of growing up is discovery of the range of life styles available to us. Through the kind of books we share with children at the top of the First School, they begin to perceive a variety of possible identities and so enrich their own self-image. This is a time when a greater depth of characterization is necessary, so we move from the flat or sketchy characters of the early stories nearer to the complexities and subtleties of real life.

Grandfather by Jeannie Baker (Deutsch)
Relationships across the generations, as the girl finds grandfather's untidy shop fascinating, his kindness comforting. The short text and collage pictures make the book accessible to readers with little fluency.

Mary of Mile 18 by Ann Blades (Bodley Head)
Winter in an isolated community in north-west Canada, based on Ann Blades's own experience as a teacher at Mile 18. Chosen as Book of the Year for Children by the Canadian Library Association.

The Big Flood in the Bush by Ruth Dallas (Methuen)
One of Methuen's Read Aloud books, intended for First School readers, and set in New Zealand of the 1890s. A traditional family story, with skilful mother and resourceful children working together to combat a natural disaster. In the same series are two warm, unassuming stories by Geraldine Kaye: *Kassim Goes Fishing*, with a Malay background, and *Kofi and the Eagle*, a touching story of a West Indian boy.

Little Bear's Journey by Evelyn Davies (H. Hamilton)
Evelyn Davies has written several stories in the Antelope series dealing with American Indian or pioneer events. This one takes the classic theme of the journey through which the hero has to prove himself, and offers us a model of courage and selflessness.

The Chief's Daughter by Rosemary Sutcliff (H. Hamilton)
Sutcliff's tone of high drama in a gripping tale of a primitive Welsh tribe and their Irish captor.

Social values

It is usual for commentators to note that fiction reflects the values of its times. It would perhaps be more accurate to say that it reflects the values of its writers. Some of these will have values which match those generally current, but the didactic writers will be ahead of their times, trying to move society on to a new stage rather than to comment on its present state. Currently, several groups and individuals connected with children's books are seeking to bring about such a change. Their desire is to create a society freed of prejudice, and their particular concern is bias of three kinds – on grounds of class, race and sex. In fact, the political and social history of the twentieth century does show a gradual progress in all these fields, but this very progress has brought problems to book selectors. Past writers reflected the standards of their times, and, when these are no longer acceptable, do we reject their books, however highly regarded in literary terms? Helen Bannerman's *Little Black Sambo* and Hugh Lofting's *Dr Dolittle* books, for example, are immediate targets for those who see children's books in social rather than literary terms. Naturally, such reassessment has been challenged, and for an introduction to the argument one can read Brian Alderson's article 'Banning Bannerman'[44] with Janet Hill's response, 'Oh! Please Mr Tiger'[45].

Since the early 1970s the campaign has changed its emphasis. Although existing books are still tried and condemned, the main effort is directed to promoting publication of books which do present acceptable attitudes. One can point to the institution in 1975 of **The Other Award** by the Children's Rights Workshop, with the aim of highlighting 'books that make a contribution to the development of a children's literature that reflects our changing society', to the production of selection guidelines, such as John Vincent's in 'Bias in Children's Books'[46], and the issue of a review journal, *Children's Book Bulletin*, edited by Rosemary Stones and published by Children's Rights Workshop. Again, moves such as that of the Librarians for Social Change to influence publication to 'try and control . . . the more despicable manifestations of injustices such as racism, sexism and ageism' have envinced a strong response, witness Bernard Levin's attack on such semi-censorship in *The Times* of May 30 and 31, 1978.

Children's books, and especially stories, have been used as carriers of messages for centuries, as Gillian Avery's survey, *Childhood's Pattern*[47], makes clear, but at different periods either freedom or didacticism has come to the fore. Current didactic pressures are obvious, as many critics have noted. Sheila Egoff[48], for example, writing in 1969, found that children's books were concerned with social issues 'to a degree not known since the seventeenth century', and Frank Eyre, in his study *British Children's Books in the Twentieth Century*[49], reached a similar conclusion. 'We can now see trends towards a new kind of didacticism. Many of these books are honest in purpose and performance, but most have a slightly unnatural air.' He found children's books subject to greater scrutiny than ever before, and authors hard put to resist pressures to write in currently fashionable ways. Publishers are under similar pressures and here, too, views on their attitudes differ. We have the Librarians for Social Change, as noted above, criticizing publishers for their bias, and Marnie Hodgkin[50], affirming on behalf of publishers, 'I think that all of us realise that there is a responsibility here, but I think it is being met and will increasingly be met, and as the world changes, so books will reflect it'.

It is unlikely that any teacher will want to choose books which present a biased view of life, or which are likely to cause offence. The basic issue, however, is rather that of selection criteria. Do we choose books because of their value in promoting a fair society, or for their intrinsic literary value? This issue is one of current importance on which each professional dealing with children's reading should have an opinion, and these opinions should receive expression in the school or library's book policy. Consideration of the articles and books noted below may help in the formulation of that policy.

Sexism in Children's Books papers . . . edited by the Children's Rights Workshop. (Writers & Readers Publishing Co-operative 1976) Subtitled: A collection of introductory articles on sexism in children's literature.
Contents:

Sex-role socialisation in picture books for preschool children

An 'examination of prize-winning picture books reveal that women are greatly under-represented in the titles, central roles and illustrations'. The books chosen were winners of the American Library Association's Caldecott medal.

Sexism in award winning picture books

Extracts from an American thesis of 1972. The author claims to show that 'children's books are not only sexist in their under-representation of females, but also in recent years they have become more, not less sexist'.

Sex-roles in reading schemes

An analysis of the characters, and the activities assigned to them, in some British reading schemes. The author accepts that the 'major premise underlying the current debate about class and race bias in reading schemes is that the content of the schemes influences children's attitudes to the world and themselves', but does not provide evidence to support the premise.

The McGraw-Hill guidelines

Guidelines issued by an American publishing company to ensure equal treatment of the sexes by authors and editors.

Non-sexist Picture Books compiled and produced by CISSY, 1979.
A list of recommended books, with annotations which emphasize the group's interests, eg, John Burningham's *Cannonball Simp* (Cape) is introduced as a 'story about an unattractive and unwanted bitch'; Virginia Lee Burton's *Calico the Wonder Horse* (Faber) as about the 'brilliance, courage and unfailing optimism of a female Horse' who 'in spite of being owned by a man . . . shows total independence'.
Catching them Young by Bob Dixon (Pluto Press 1977)
Dixon, in this two-volume work, takes as his starting point: 'Much of the material in children's books is anti-social, if not anti-human, and is more likely to stunt and warp young people than help them grow'. Volume 1 deals with sex, race and class, which Dixon believes 'are undeniably the most fundamental aspects of children's fiction'. Volume 2 considers the attitudes current in comics, fantasy, adventure stories, and the work of Enid Blyton. Apart from a bibliography of sources, the author provides an unannotated list of 100 recommended children's books.
Children's Books and Class Society by Robert Leeson (Writers & Readers Publishing Cooperative 1977)
Two papers edited by the Children's Rights Workshop. In the first, a historical survey, Leeson concludes that 'the dominant values, background, atmosphere and mood' in children's literature is that of the middle class, and calls for 'the achievement of a universal literature to reflect the drive to remove social distinctions and exploitation'. The second paper, 'What are we arguing about', considers, without any clear conclusions, how far writers should respond to 'pressure to produce children's books free of the old assumptions'. It is of particular interest in setting out Leeson's own rules:
'A novel is about people, not problems: What a book has to say (its message?) should come out in the action rather than the statement: Love thine enemy, at least to the extent of letting him act out his case: There are no simple choices.' This is a book which serves to bridge gaps rather than create divides, emphasizing the middle ground, but failing to make clear some of the major points of contention. A short, unannotated list of recommended children's books is included.

It is noticeable that more writing can be found attacking the social values portrayed in children's books than questioning the movement's efforts. Through *Children's Books Abstracts* one can trace a growing trickle, for example, Carmel Kelly's 'It's a little too nice in counter-sexist fairyland' (*National Times*, 388, 15 July 1978, 27–31), a critical examination of books published by Australian feminist groups, or Jessica Kemball-Cook's 'Male chauvinist lions' (*Mallorn*, 11, 1978, 14–19), a defence of Tolkien and Lewis from charges of sexism. A consistent supporter of literary values has been John Rowe Townsend, and he alludes to the issue in *A Sounding of Storytellers* (Kestrel 1979). 'The atmosphere in which children's literature is discussed has changed since 1971. A good deal of recent comment appears to be based on the assumption that children's books are tools for shaping attitudes. Traditional literary values are dismissed as inappropriate or inadequate.' Townsend goes on to make his own position quite clear: 'To look at children's books from a narrowly restricted viewpoint as means to non-literary ends is derogatory both to them and to the whole body of literature of which they form part'.

Much of the skirmishing is on peripheral issues, and avoids the basic question of the effect of books, a point underlined by Pauline Gough in 'Non-sexist literature for children: a panacea?' (*Top of the News*, 33, Summer 1977, 334–343), on our inability to measure the effect of books in influencing attitudes.

References

For the reader's convenience the references to children's books have been separated from the academic references.

Academic

1. Godley, E. 'A century of children's books', *The National Review*, XLVII (May 1906) 437–49
2. Dixon, J. *Growth through English* (Oxford University Press for the National Association for the Teaching of English 1967)
3. Alderson, B. 'The irrelevance of children to the children's book reviewer', *Children's Book News*, 2 (Jan–Feb 1969) 10–11
4. Meek, M. 'Choosers for children', *Books*, 359 (May–June 1965) 86–90
5. Iser, W. *The Implied Reader* (Baltimore, Johns Hopkins Press 1975)
6. Iser, W. *The Act of Reading* (Routledge 1978)
7. *op. cit.*[1]
8. Townsend, J.R. 'Didacticism in modern dress', *The Horn Book Magazine*, XLIII (April 1967) 159–64
9. Aiken, J. 'Purely for love', *Books*, 365 (Winter 1970) 9–21
10. *Signal: Approaches to Children's Books* (Thimble Press)
    Children's Literature in Education (Ward Lock Educational)
11. Egoff, S. *and others. Only Connect* (New York, Oxford University Press 1969)
    Haviland, V. *Children and Literature* (Bodley Head 1973)
    Meek, M. *and others. The Cool Web* (Bodley Head 1977)
21. Department of Education & Science *A Language for Life* Bullock Report (HMSO 1975)
28. Jones, A. & Mulford, J. (Ed) *Children Using Language* (Oxford University Press 1971)

32. Lewis, C.S. 'On stories' in Lewis, C.S. (Ed) *Essays Presented to Charles Williams* (Oxford University Press 1947)
33. Hardy, B. *Tellers and Listeners* (Athlone Press 1975)
34. Whitehead, F. *and others. Children's Reading Interests* (Evans/Methuen Educational 1975)
35. Berg, L. *Reading and Loving* (Routledge & Kegan Paul 1977)
36. Harding, D.W. 'Psychological processes in the reading of fiction', *British Journal of Aesthetics*, 2 (1962) 133–47
37. Tolkien, J.R.R. *Tree and Leaf* (Allen and Unwin 1964)
38. Rosen, C. & Rosen, H. *The Language of Primary School Children* (Penguin Education 1973)
39. *op. cit.*[6]
41. Durell, A. 'The best book I ever read', *The Horn Book Magazine*, LV (April 1979) 161–9
42. Isaacs, N. *The Growth of Understanding in the Young Child: A Brief Introduction to Piaget's Work* (Ward Lock 1961)
43. Leng, I.J. *Children in the Library* (Cardiff, University of Wales Press 1968)
44. Alderson, B. 'Banning Bannerman', *The Times* (12 April 1972)
45. Hill, J. 'Oh! Please Mr Tiger', *The Times Literary Supplement* (3 Nov 1972)
46. Vincent, J. 'Bias in children's books', *Assistant Librarian*, 69 (April 1976) 68–70
47. Avery, G. *Childhood's Pattern* (Hodder 1975)
48. *op. cit.*[11]
49. Eyre, F. *British Children's Books in the Twentieth Century* (Longman 1971)
50. Discussion reported in *CISSY Talks to Publishers* (CISSY 1974)

Children's books

12. Arthur, F. *Captain Rocco Rides to Sheffield* (Chatto)
13. Hughes, T. *The Iron Man* (Faber)
14. Mahy, M. *The Great Piratical Rumbustification* (Dent)
15. Pearce, P. *A Dog So Small* (Longman)
16. Keeping, C. *Charlie, Charlotte and the Golden Canary* (Oxford University Press)
17. Swindells, R. *The Ice Palace* (H. Hamilton)
18. Hoban, R. *How Tom Beat Captain Najork and his Hired Sportsmen* (Cape)
19. McDonald, J. *Maggy Scraggle Loves the Beautiful Ice-cream Man* (Kestrel)
20. Edwards, D. *My Naughty Little Sister* (Methuen)
22. Sendak, M. *Where the Wild Things Are* (Bodley Head)
23. Boston, L. *The Sea Egg* (Faber)
24. Vestly, A.C. *Eight Children and a Truck* (Methuen)
25. Mahy, M. *The Man whose Mother was a Pirate* (Dent)
26. Blyton, D. *The Rat-a-tat Mystery* (Collins)
27. Pemberton, P.D. *Richard's M-Class Cows* (Faber)
29. Cutler, I. *Meal One* (Heinemann)
30. Hughes, S. *It's Too Frightening for Me* (Hodder)
31. Benchley, N. *The Magic Sledge* (Deutsch)
40. Hutchins, P. *Rosie's Walk* (Bodley Head)

Selection aids

Bibliographies go out of date quickly and are of limited help. The best guide to selection is one's own judgment, trained through exercise and discussion, and backed by a sense of purpose. Consideration and criticism of the children's books noted in this chapter will help in building up such expertise. The following sources are valuable in signposting other stories one may wish to buy, borrow, and share with children.

Children's Stories compiled by Berna Clark (School Library Association 1974)

A list of fiction, poetry and picture books for children in Primary and Middle Schools, with brief annotations for each title. It is difficult to prescribe cut-off points for particular stories, and several of the books recommended here for 'younger juniors' will be suitable for First School pupils.

Intent upon Reading by Margery Fisher, 2nd edn (Hodder 1964)

The earlier chapters deal with stories of domesticity, talking animals, and aspects of fantasy. Each chapter contains discussion and description of recommended books and a reading list.

Carry on Reading by Jo Kemp (National Book League 1975)

An annotated list of books suitable for children who have just learned to read.

Children's Paperbacks, 5–11 by Margaret Marshall (National Book League with the School Library Association 1978)

Fifteen recommendations for 5–7 year olds, and a further seventy for 8–12 age group. The long annotations are very helpful in conveying the flavour of each book.

Reading for Enjoyment for 6 to 8 Year Olds by Joan & Alan Tucker (Children's Booknews Ltd 1975)

A booklist with an individual character, the choice of titles supported by long, enthusiastic annotations. Interesting to compare with the earlier edition of the list, compiled by Brian Alderson in 1970.

Also helpful are the very practical publications of the ILEA's Centre for Language in Primary Education.

5

Traditional tales

Contents

Great survivors
The language development model
The cultural heritage model
Personal development

Versions to choose
References
Selection aids

Great survivors

Few literary forms have received such a mixture of adulation and attack as folk and fairy tales. These stories, which were originally part of an adult oral culture, were among the chapman's best-selling lines. They received abuse from eighteenth century rationalists and nineteenth century moralists. They were blamed as a cause of Nazi insensitivity, and today are regarded as a valuable educational tool, bearing a Bullock seal of approval. Indeed, the Report recommends that 'fantasy, fairy tale and folk tale should take their place in the repertoire in the earliest stages of reading' because they 'contain the strength and simplicity of their origins, as well as their deep significance'. We can trace the early history of traditional tales in works such as Harvey Darton's *Children's Books in England*[1], and read of their struggle for survival in Paul Hazard's *Books, Children and Men*[2]. From the Opies' *The Classic Fairy Tales*[3] and Bruno Bettelheim's *The Uses of Enchantment*[4] we can discover the drastic changes in plot and character which have occurred over the years. For example, the transition from she-fox to human vixen and thence to pretty Goldilocks in 'The Three Bears', and the removal from Cinderella of a whole sequence in which our heroine murders one step-mother before being oppressed by a second. At times well-wishers have rewritten these old stories to incorporate desirable features or remove disturbing ones. So we can find a nineteenth century Puss in Boots calling for milk at the King's court with the explanation that 'on principle he was a teetotaller'[5], or a recent Red Riding Hood in which the repentant wolf 'gave up trying to eat people' and took up vegetable gardening instead[6]. Stories of foolish peasants, selfish princesses, wicked fairies and ruthless soldiers – what, looked at in the light of Dixon's three models set out in Chapter 1, have these patched tales to do with today's children?

The language development model

It would be pedantic to impose a classification on stories with such a changing history, but one can see many different kinds of story sheltering under the umbrella term 'traditional tales'. They include the humble folk tale of unknown origin, the elaborate courtly romances of Perrault, primitive myths and hero legends, and a train of modern stories in traditional mode, running from Andersen to Aiken. Each of these will have an appropriate pace and style, and in sharing them with children we shall be widening the range of language at their disposal.

There is the rustic simplicity of tales born of poverty and the struggle to find food:

'In a little hut near the edge of a deep, deep forest lived a poor woodchopper with his wife and his two children, Hansel and Gretel. Times were hard. Work was scarce and the price of food was high. Many people were starving, and our poor woodchopper and his little brood fared as badly as all the rest'[7].

Perrault's tales are aglitter with scenes and fancies to please his late seventeenth century audience which had wearied of the classical and turned for entertainment to the fabulous. Even in translations of his *Histoires ou Contes du Temps Passé* we catch something of the confidence and style of this society:

'So sleep fell upon the enchanted castle and upon all within it, because of the Princess Briar-Rose, who lay there on her couch in the ancient tower waiting till the hundred years should be past and the Prince should come to waken her. And all round the castle there grew up a hedge of thorn, tangled with ivy, woodbine and creeping plants, so dense that from a distance it seemed like a little wood'[8].

With Hans Andersen we are in very different territory. By the intensity of his imagination he built settings of beauty, splendour and strange power, but they are inhabited by beings capable of the deepest pain and most faithful love. There is no question that the reader will not enter these scenes as readily as the author, for every detail is depicted vividly and we are drawn swiftly into this unpredictable world, compounded of the miraculous and the sinister.

'So now she knew where the prince lived and it was there she went many an evening and night. She would swim much closer to the land than any of her sisters had ventured to. She even dared to swim up to the small canal beneath the splendid marble balcony which cast a long shadow over the water, and here she would sit and gaze upon the young prince, who believed he was all alone in the bright moonlight'[9].

The high tone of medieval romance is sounded in the hero legends of Arthur and Tristan, Gawain and Roland:

'Gawain endured all – foes to overcome, and the bitter weather of mid-winter. On Christmas Eve he rode upon Gringalet through marsh and mire, and prayed that he might find shelter. And on a sudden he came through open parkland to a fine castle set on a little hill above a deep valley where flowed a wide stream. A fair lawn lay in front of it, and many great oak trees on either side; there was a moat before the castle, and a low palisade of wood. "Now God be thanked" said Sir Gawain, "that I have come to this fair dwelling for Christmas"'[10].

If one had to find one style typical of traditional tales, it would be the spare language of the majority of folk tales which, by its very matter-of-factness, persuades readers to believe in the spells, witches, talking animals and magical adventures. Among modern writers, Isaac Bashevis Singer fits exactly into the folk tale tradition, and Joan Aiken has the style in her bones, as the invented tales in *Necklace of Raindrops* show. James Reeves and Walter de la Mare brought the poet's view of language to the folk tale. Reeves's dialogue is simple, even stilted, but in the descriptive passages the rhythm and pacing are sure. As for De la Mare, he would have been hard put to write a clumsy or banal sentence: his stories in the traditional mode offer the listener continuing pleasure in the cadences of the beautifully balanced sentences. Here is his opening to 'Cinderella and the Glass Slipper':

'There were once upon a time three sisters who lived in an old, high, stone house not very far from the great square of the city where was the palace of the King. The two eldest of these sisters were old and ugly, which is bad enough. They were also sour and jealous, which is worse. And simply because the youngest (who was only their half-sister) was gentle and lovely, they hated her'[11].

Whatever the variation, the traditional tale, by its very age, is different from the everyday present, and its language signals the distinction. The slight period flavour, the idiomatic turns of phrase, the use of refrains, even the conventional openings – 'Once upon a time' or 'In the olden times, when wishing still helped' – command attention. These are not stories of little Pete and his tricycle: they are stories dredged from antiquity, steeped in magic, and as such they demand a language different from classroom or home.

The discipline imposed by an oral tradition has ensured a simple plot line for most folk tales. Going back to the point in *Children Using Language*[12] about appreciation of form being one of the major satisfactions of fiction, we can see that these stories offer an early illustration of the shape of narrative: the exposition, the adventure undertaken, the conclusion. A recurring device is that of the thrice-repeated event, with a variation in the third attempt – seen, for example, in 'The Golden Bird', or 'The Three Little Pigs'. Children enjoy the security of the repetition, the pleasure of anticipation, the swing away on the third occasion. In their turn, fairy tales offer models for children's own storying, having an effect on the content and shape of their daydreams, talk, and written work. Both Ralph Lavender[13] and Margaret Spencer[14] provide examples of such influence, but much classroom work offers similar illustration of the relationship between stories presented and the child's creativity.

The cultural heritage model

It is strange to realize that many of the stories regarded in England as 'traditional' are in fact from Germanic sources, or with connections dating back to Louis XIV's court. 'Red Riding Hood', 'Puss in Boots', 'Hop o' my Thumb' and 'Cinderella' were among Perrault's tales; 'Rumpelstiltskin', 'The Goosegirl', 'The Twelve Dancing Princesses' were among the Grimm Brothers' collection. The major collection of English stories was that of Joseph Jacobs, 1890 – dismissed by one literary historian[15] as 'addressed more to anthropologists and folk-lorists than to children' – which gave wider circulation to native tales like 'Mr Fox' and 'Jack and the Beanstalk'. Jacobs's *English Fairy Tales* have been reissued by Bodley Head, and can be supplemented by collections from other parts of the British Isles in, for example, editions from Bodley Head and Oxford University Press. Also available are one-volume gatherings of national tales, for example, *British Fairy Tales*, retold by Amabel Williams-Ellis (Blackie).

Stories are no respectors of national boundaries though. We can find similar stories appearing in many different countries – for example Tom Thumb variants appear in England, France and Norway; Perrault's Cinderella is Grimm's Aschenputtel; Bluebeard has counterparts in at least three countries. Yet, although these versions may have a similar plot line, the atmosphere and characters will reflect the country of origin. Folk tales are bound up with ideas of national identity and codes of behaviour, and so can be of great help to us in developing a multi-cultural society. Whatever our immediate child audience, we are preparing children for a local society to which a range of races and nationalities contribute, and a world society in which sympathies and alliances widen and federal political structures increase in importance. Ralph Lavender sees myth and legend giving us a sense of belonging 'to the world, to mankind, and to the wisdom of accumulated experience. For the same roots are common to all men, mankind had a common beginning, and an awareness of this, it is to be hoped, might improve the quality of our social justice'. Against such a background, there is a value in giving our children experience, through story, of other cultures and conditions, and in this work we have great assistance from publishers. We can introduce the Anansi stories of African and West Indian origin through P.M. Sherlock's retellings (Macmillan), make known the *Tales of the Punjab*, collected by Flora Anne Steel in the late nineteenth century (Bodley Head); move from *Aboriginal Myths and Legends*, retold by R. Robinson (Hamlyn) to the Eastern Europe of Joan Aiken's *The Kingdom under the Sea* (Cape).

Personal development

It is the personal development aspect of traditional tales which has been most hotly disputed. 'Cinderella' encourages discontent and a taste for frivolity, 'The Three Bears' a lack of respect for other people's property – not to mention the gratuitous violence of the soldier in 'The Tinder Box', or the sadism of 'The Juniper Tree'. Even more vociferous have been the supporters of fairy tales: 'The Three Little Pigs', is a lesson in prudence; 'Snow White and Rose Red' one in kindness and hospitality. Charles Lamb, Chesterton and Dickens have been among the defenders, the latter noting 'the amount of gentleness and mercy that has made its way among us through these slight channels. Forbearance, courtesy, consideration for the poor and aged, kind treatment of animals, the love of nature, abhorrence of tyranny and brute force – many such good things have been first nourished in the child's heart by this powerful aid'[16].

Today, the sad and frightening aspect of fairy tales is not only admitted but regarded as part of their therapy. Over the last few decades we have come to a fresh understanding of the dark side of human nature, and of the role of story in helping children work through their feelings of aggression and frustration. Relevant to our thinking here is Catherine Storr's paper 'Fear and evil in children's books'[17] and Ralph Lavender's insight: 'The truth is that you and I have both dreamed of monsters; and we look to myth, legend and lore for proof that the medusas and the minotaurs are not invincible'[18]. It would, however, be misleading to dwell too much on the violence in folk tales. There is such a wealth of material available that one can avoid stories with elements regarded as disturbing. In most cases the dark aspects of folk tale are set in a context generally hopeful and positive. As J. Newby Hetherington put it 'there is a kind of real life in them, such life as a child believes in, where good is always rewarded and evil always punished'[19]. The element of ruthlessness accords with children's sense of rough justice. The characters presented are generally one-dimensional, with obvious attributes, and this meeting with the good, bad; silly, crafty; weak, courageous; helps the young reader absorb the conventions of fiction. Cinderella and Snow-White have to be long-suffering and kind; the youngest son is typecast for early ridicule and eventual success; jealous stepmothers and the whole tribe of giants, witches and trolls are consistently horrid. This simplicity of characterization permits both hero worship and the projection of feelings of hatred, a therapy documented by Joan Cass[20]. Folk tales were devised by man at a primitive stage of development, and their themes have particular appeal to children, who are at a comparable stage. Against an anthropomorphic background, in which children feel at home, are played out stories of emotional strength and simplicity. Here the boy can overcome the giant, the despised win recognition; home is a place to return to after adventures which end 'happily ever after'; the individual meets hardship but he has an opportunity to change and control his life. The wickedest witch can be beaten.

What more the old tales tell is left to each one of us to decide, with the help of a battery of experts. Bruno Bettelheim, one of these, observed that the 'literature *about* fairy tales is nearly as voluminous as that of fairy tales', and the lengthy bibliography, mostly of German studies, appended to his *The Uses of Enchantment*[21] bears out the statement. It is from reading Bettelheim that we learn that 'Little Red Riding Hood' speaks of 'human passions, oral greediness, aggression, and pubertal sexual desires'; that 'Jack and the Beanstalk' centres on phallic potency, and that Prince Charming accepts Cinderella's 'vagina in the form of the slipper, and approves of her desire for a penis, symbolized by her tiny foot fitting within the slipper-vagina'. Few of us are likely to have the scholarship or imagination to match Bettelheim at this game; some may dismiss such speculation as Andrew Lang did in the introduction to his Red Fairy Book, published in 1890: 'As specialism advances, we may see young men, spectacled from the cradle, and bald from their birth, voyage into middle age and extreme eld, still poring over Cinderella or Puss in Boots'[22]. But whether one sees Bettelheim's suggestions as revelatory or ridiculous, they indicate the levels of meaning within folk tale and help to explain its continuing fascination.

As we move to the world of myth and legend the possibilities multiply. Western society is still influenced by the Arthurian myth, and still cannot understand it. Wagnerians continue to listen to, and just fail to capture, the meanings hidden within, the Ring cycle. Myth deals with ritual and destiny and as such needs to be experienced rather than explained. It is best to present such stories to children as an emotional sequence, not as a subject for analysis – that can be left to the experts. Once more we come to the advantage of children meeting these famous tales first through the medium of the adult's voice. It is the adult telling or reading which can reveal the shape and pace of the story, the attributes of its characters, and the significance of the events.

Versions to choose

Brian Alderson once castigated teachers and librarians for choosing versions of folk tales lacking in authenticity. They brought no critical intelligence to bear in choosing editions, reacting without discrimination 'to glossy printing or smart design'[23]. Yet what can the average teacher or librarian do faced, say, with a new version of Andersen or Grimm? Without knowledge of Danish or German, access to the originals, and time to study them, how can we choose? And even if we go some way to building a critical apparatus for European folktales, we are unlikely to bring the same expertise to bear on Chinese, African or Russian tales. In the introduction to his *Myths, Legends and Lore*[24], Ralph Lavender suggests a few tests to apply. 'The spirit of the original is of prime importance: its imaginative and true re-creation, the sensitivity of the language employed, the living of the book, and the freshness of a sense of wonder are all criteria one hopes to find satisfied.' Yet even this advice will often be difficult to apply. We are rarely equipped to know the original so well that we can judge the survival of its essence.

The answer has got to be much simpler. It must lie in a careful reading of the text on offer, an assessment of its illustration, and recourse to the sources of expert help which are readily available, i.e. reviews and bibliographies. It is true that many indifferent versions of famous stories are published each year, and we can waste a great deal of public money – quite apart from the loss to our children – by buying the poor rather than the good. It is worthwhile trying to establish, through local workshops or study groups, a recommended list, some selection guidelines, or some touchstones in the form of distinguished work. When a new single story is published in picture book form, it is sensible to set it against standard translations. While Alderson, in the article quoted above, seemed hostile to the idea of picture book versions (recognising 'the power of these texts to evoke their own pictures without interference from designers'), this may be a better way to introduce them in the classroom or library than via the 'large and properly severe' tomes Alderson recommends. This is where selection must be accompanied by some ideas about use. In particular, we need to decide whether we will tell or read the stories, and whether the books are for teachers' or children's use.

An almost unique aid to the selection of traditional tales is Elizabeth Cook's *The Ordinary and the Fabulous*[25]. This thought-provoking book is forthright in its assessment of much current educational practice, challenging in its belief in the value of stories. Elizabeth Cook's thesis is that 'fabulous stories illuminate the ordinary world'. She sets out to show that 'understanding of life is incomplete without an understanding of myths, legends and fairy tales; that the process of growing up would be harder and drearier without them; that there is an abundance of fabulous stories that are enjoyed by children of different ages and that there are innumerable ways of presenting them so that they become part and parcel of children's lives'. The first section of the book sets out the significance and value of these stories. The second is a description of the major legends – Greek myths, Norse tales, Arthurian legends etc. The following section gives suggestions for their presentation in the classroom, and the fourth is a critical comparison of different editions or translations of key scenes from seven well-known stories. Lastly, comes a 50 page annotated book list of versions suitable for children.

Elizabeth Cook concentrates on the 8–14 age group – a deliberate choice since she considers that 'many of the best fairy tales are not stories for very young children'. Nevertheless, her book is to be recommended to anyone interested in presenting traditional tales to children. Many of the titles in the book list are suitable for First Schools; the first section has a general application, and the fourth section must improve the book selection techniques of all who read it, helping them become more aware of the atmosphere of each story, and more sensitive to the language needed to convey that atmosphere.

The titles listed below illustrate the range of traditional tales available, and an appropriate level of presentation, faithful to the mode of the traditional tale and accessible to children. They may also be useful in selection workshops, in conjunction with the titles noted under *Workshop Comparisons*.

Recommended titles

Anthologies

Stories for Seven-Year Olds selected by Sarah & Stephen Corrin,
    illustrated by Shirley Hughes (Faber)
A modest collection which serves as an introduction to the work of Andersen and Grimm. The same editors have produced *Stories for Six-Year-Olds*, which has some of the simplest traditional tales such as

'The Gingerbread Boy', and modern stories in the same vein, and *Stories for Eight-Year-Olds*, which introduces some of the hero legends.

Tales from Grimm freely translated and illustrated by Wanda Gag (Faber)

A vigorous version, with clear associations with the peasant oral tradition.

The Fairy Tale Treasury selected by Virginia Haviland and illustrated by Raymond Briggs, (H. Hamilton)

A bumper book of thirty two stories, drawn mainly from Perrault, Grimm, and Andersen. Valuable as a source book for storytelling, as well as a browsing book for children. See also Haviland's shorter collections for Bodley Head, e.g. *Favourite Fairy Tales Told in England*.

The Ten Minute Story Book selected by Kathleen Lines, illustrated by Winifred Marks (Oxford University Press)

The selection, by a distinguished editor, of simple nursery tales, which establish the folk tale conventions.

Folk Tales from North America retold by Peter Lum, illustrated by John Spender (Muller)

The American Indians' view of the creation of the world, together with nature myths and fables. Not intended specifically for First School children, but offering a new direction for more mature pupils.

A Book of Dragons by Ruth Manning-Sanders, illustrated by Robin Jacques (Methuen)

One of a series of folk tale collections written in a colloquial style, suitable for reading aloud. Quite complex plots for First School audiences, but little to frighten. *A Choice of Magic* is a gathering of Ruth Manning-Sanders's favourites from previous collections, and, as such, provides an introduction to stories from many cultures.

Heroes and Monsters by James Reeves, illustrated by Sarah Nechamkin (Blackie)

A plain rendering of some of the major hero legends, including tales of Icarus, Orpheus, Persephone, Prometheus and Theseus.

The Secret Shoemakers and Other Stories adapted by James Reeves, illustrated by Edward Ardizzone (Abelard)

Some of the well-known Grimm stories are included in an easy, colloquial translation.

Single stories

Several picture book versions are noted in Chapter 3 also.

The Green Children retold by Kevin Crossley-Holland, illustrated by Margaret Gordon (Macmillan)

Crossley-Holland makes this haunting story his own, keeping all the mystery, and the pain of loyalties to two worlds. Powerful illustrations.

The Miller, His Son and Their Donkey retold and illustrated by Roger Duvoisin (Bodley Head)

A reworking of Aesop's fable about the miller beset by good advice. Text and pictures make the most of the humour of the situations.

The Fisherman and His Wife translated by Margaret Hunt and illustrated by Katrin Brandt (Bodley Head)

A Grimm story well suited to First School children by virtue of its clear story line, repeated elements and inevitable end.

The Emperor's New Clothes by Hans Christian Andersen, pictures by Monika Laimgruber (H. Hamilton)

Witty illustrations point up the text, which follows closely Andersen's original, although no translator is named.

King Arthur's Sword by Errol Le Cain (Faber)

Rich, stylised illustrations with medieval overtones provide an apt setting for this single story from the Arthurian romances. A sophisticated treatment.

Cinderella retold by Kathleen Lines, illustrated by Shirely Hughes (Bodley Head)

An honest version, based on Robert Samber's eighteenth century translation of Perrault, with warm illustrations fitting the period. One of a distinguished series, Bodley Head Fairy Tale Picture Books.

Anansi the Spider retold and illustrated by Gerald McDermott (H. Hamilton)

A striking picture book, adapted from a film sequence, which takes one of the tales of the Ashanti legends about the cunning spider-man.

Maui and the Big Fish retold and illustrated by Katarina Mataira (Angus & Robertson)

A touching Maori folk tale about a youngest son with a gift of magic. The dramatic pictures are in the tradition of Maori folk art.

The Hare and the Tortoise retold and illustrated by Brian Wildsmith (Oxford University Press)

Bold colour work and a simple retelling of Aesop's well-known fable.

Nail Soup retold by Harve Zemach, pictures by Margot Zemach (Blackie)

A robust rendering of an amusing Swedish tale about a mean woman and a clever tramp. A very simple story line.

Workshop comparisons

At an early stage selectors need to decide which editions of major fairy tale collectors or writers to choose. In this process one needs to compare the renderings of individual stories in several versions, considering which teller best conveys the mood of the story and the

shape of the plot. The following examples are designed mere
illustrate the method, which has been developed and refine
Elizabeth Cook.

The Wild Swans by Hans Andersen
Which opening best conveys the mood of this romantic story of
faithful love?

Seven Stories by Hans Christian Andersen illustrated and retold by Eric
  Carle (Franklin Watts)

> 'In a distant land there lived a king and his queen. They had twelve
> children – eleven boys and a girl, Elisa, who was the youngest. They
> all loved each other very much and had a happy time together. One
> day the queen became ill. All ʾhe doctors were called in, but they
> could not help her. She died . . .'

Hans Andersen's Fairy Tales illustrated by Rene Cloke (Ward Lock)

> 'Long ago, there was once a King who had eleven fine sons and one
> lovely daughter, the fair Elise. They all lived very happily together,
> until the widowed King remarried a Queen from a distant land . . .'

Hans Andersen: His Classic Fairy Tales translated by Erik Haugaard,
  illustrated by Michael Foreman (Gollancz)

> 'Far, far away where the swallows are when we have winter, there
> lived a king who had eleven sons and one daughter, Elisa. The
> eleven brothers were all princes; and when they went to school,
> each wore a star on his chest and a sword at his side. They wrote
> with diamond pencils on golden tablets, and read aloud so beauti-
> fully that everyone knew at once that they were of royal blood.
> Their sister Elisa sat on a little stool made of mirrors and had a
> picture book that had cost half the kingdom. How well those
> children lived; but it did not last . . .'

The Emperor's New Clothes by Hans Andersen
The opening of this satirical tale of a rich man's folly in M.R. James's
1930 translation and a recent picture book version.

Favourite Tales of Hans Andersen translated by M.R. James (Faber)

> 'Many years ago there lived an Emperor who was so monstrous fond
> of fine new clothes that he spent all his money on being really smart.
> He didn't care about his army, he didn't care for going to the play,
> or driving out in the park, unless it was to show his new clothes. He
> had a coat for every hour in the day; and just as people say about a
> king, that "he's holding a council", so in this country they always
> said, "The Emperor is in his dressing room . . ."'

The Emperor's New Clothes adapted . . . by Fulvio Testa (Abelard)

> 'Many years ago two strangers arrived in the Kingdom. They had

heard of an Emperor who was excessively fond of clothes. Pretending to be weavers, they came to offer him samples of their work. When the strangers arrived at the palace, the Emperor was in his dressing room as usual, dreaming of clothes. It was widely known that he spent more time there than in his council chamber . . .'

The Fisherman and his Wife from the Brothers Grimm
This peasant tale of a discontented wife has a rough humour and something of the satisfaction of a cumulative tale, with its sequence of ever more unreasonable demands. Here are the closing paragraphs of two recent translations.

The Brothers Grimm: Popular Folk Tales translated by Brian Alderson, illustrated by Michael Foreman (Gollancz)

'But the storm was raging something terrible and blowing so he could scarcely stand on his two feet. Trees and houses were tumbling down, the hills were shaking and bits of rock were crashing into the sea. The heavens were black as pitch; there was thunder and lightning, and the sea hurled up waves as high as steeples and mountains, all crowned with caps of white foam. So he called – and could never hear his own words:

"Mannikin, mannikin, timpe tee
Flounder, flounder in the sea
My old missis Ilsebill
Will not have it as I will."

"Well, what does she want now?" said the flounder. "Aw" said he, "she wants to be like the good Lord himself." "Go on home" said the flounder, "she's sitting in the piss-pot again." And there they stayed sitting until this very day.'

Grimms' Tales for Young and Old the complete stories translated by Ralph Manheim (Gollancz)

'A storm was raging. The wind was blowing so hard he could hardly keep his feet. Trees and houses were falling, the mountains were trembling, great boulders were tumbling into the sea, the sky was as black as pitch, the thunder roared, the lightning flashed, the sea was rising up in great black waves as big as mountains and church towers, and each one had a crown of foam on top. He couldn't hear his own words, but he shouted:

"Little man, whoever you be,
Flounder, flounder in the sea,
My wife, her name is Ilsebil,
Has sent me here against my will."

"Well, what does she want?" asked the flounder. "Dear me," he said, "she wants to be like God." "Just go home, she's back in the old pigsty already." And there they are living to this day.'

References

1. Darton, F.J.H. *Children's Books in England: Five Centuries of Social Life* (Cambridge University Press 1958)
2. Hazard, P. *Books, Children and Men* (Boston [Mass], The Horn Book Inc. 1947)
3. Opie, I. & Opie P. *The Classic Fairy Tales* (Oxford University Press 1974)
4. Bettelheim, B. *The Uses of Enchantment: the Meaning and Importance of Fairy Tales* (Thames & Hudson 1976)
5. Baring-Gould, S. *A Book of Fairy Tales* (Methuen 1894)
6. Ross, T. *Little Red Riding Hood* (Andersen Press 1978)
7. Gag, W. *Tales from Grimm* (Faber 1937)
8. Evans, C.S. *The Sleeping Beauty* (Heinemann 1920)
9. Corrin, S. *translator. Ardizzone's Hans Andersen* (Deutsch 1978)
10. Green, R. *King Arthur and his Knights of the Round Table* (Penguin 1953)
11. De la Mare, W. *Tales Told Again* (Faber 1959)
12. Jones, A. & Mulford, J. (Ed) *Children Using Language* (Oxford University Press for the National Association for the Teaching of English 1971)
13. Lavender, R. *Myths, Legend and Lore* (Blackwell 1975)
14. *op. cit.*[12]
15. Muir, P. *English Children's Books: 1600 to 1900* (Batsford 1954)
16. Dickens, C. 'Frauds on the fairies', *Household Words*, 184 (Oct 1853)
17. Storr, C. 'Fear and evil in children's books', *Children's Literature in Education*, (March 1970) 22–40
18. *op. cit.*[13]
19. Hetherington, J.N. 'The use of fairy tales in the education of the young', *The Journal of Education*, XIX (Aug 1897) 472–74
20. Cass, J. *Literature and the Young Child* (Longmans 1967)
21. *op. cit.*[4]
22. Lang, A. *The Red Fairy Book* (Longmans 1890)
23. Alderson, B. 'When wishing still helped . . .', *The Times Educational Supplement* (24 Nov 1978) 39
24. *op. cit.*[13]
25. Cook, E. *The Ordinary and the Fabulous* 2nd edn (Cambridge University Press 1976)

Selection aids

The major guide is Elizabeth Cook's *The Ordinary and the Fabulous*, already discussed in this chapter. While the main text establishes criteria, a range of annotated booklists provides a quick checklist to recommended titles. Most of the books listed are for the Junior or Middle School age-group, but some attention is paid to picture book versions and anthologies suitable for First School pupils. Ralph Lavender's *Myths, Legend and Lore*, also already mentioned, is another valuable guide. The greater part of the book is given to seven annotated lists, six of books and one of audio-visual material: List One has about a dozen items, mainly picture books and rhymes suggested for First Schools; List Two about twenty-five simple retellings; List Three contains over one hundred tales and folk collections, some of which can be used at the top of the First School; List Seven has films,

filmstrips and music which will appeal to a wide age-range. Biblio-
graphical details are sufficient for identification but much briefer than
Cook's, while the annotations are descriptive rather than evaluative.
Supplementary sources include:

Intent upon Reading by Margery Fisher 2nd ed, (Hodder 1964)
Chapter Five, The Land of Faerie, is given to discussion of old and
new tales in the folk tale mode: an unannotated reading list is
included. While many of the stories noted, for example works by
George Macdonald, C.S. Lewis and Tolkien, are not intended for
First Schools, the chapter does provide a background for thoughts on
traditional tales and some appropriate recommendations.

Reading for Enjoyment for 6 to 8 Year-Olds by Joan & Alan
    Tucker (Children's Booknews Ltd 1975)
This booklist, already noted in Chapter 4, contains a number of
traditional tales among its recommendations.

Children's Books of the Year produced annually by Hamish Hamilton
in association with the National Book League, usually contains a
separate section on myths and legends. The list is only a selection of
quality books of each year, but it affords a way of checking outstanding new publications.

6

Finding the facts

Contents

The child's need to know
The books available
Making a choice
The potential of project work
The reference collection

References
Booklist
Workshop comparisons
Selection aids

The child's need to know

The need to know is a basic characteristic of all human beings, but it is particularly keen in the early years. It is a drive which provides motivation for learning in both the practical and intellectual spheres. The young child's need to know is closely bound up with his need for security. There are so many things which he does not understand, and he senses early the power which knowledge gives him over his environment. That perceptive observer, Kornei Chukovsky[1], rightly called the child a 'tireless explorer', with a burning need to take the measure of the world and search out its elements of coherence.

It is through this inbuilt curiosity that children make progress. In the immediate pre-school years their ideas of distance, time, volume, etc, are in a state of flux. As Piaget found, there is the beginning of a notable change around five to six years when, gradually, some understanding of these concepts, and of cause and effect, begins to emerge. Around the age of seven or eight children become increasingly able to reason objectively and consistently about concrete phenomenon. These are natural developments, but the adult can do much to assist and support them.

For the school, this means providing resources to satisfy the desire for knowledge. However, the matter is not so simple that it can be settled by investing in a row of reference books. Nor is it a question of just telling children facts. Mr Gradgrind, of Dickens' *Hard Times*, insisted: 'Teach these boys and girls nothing but Facts. Facts alone are wanted in life'. In this novel, written over a century ago, Gradgrind's educational views are presented as rigid and old-fashioned. Today, we should certainly realize that knowing the facts is not the same as understanding them. Many children do enjoy just collecting facts – as the popularity of *The Guinness Book of Records* shows. However, knowledge consists of more than assembling, or even remembering, facts. It includes understanding the significance of these facts. Having accepted the distinction, we next need to consider how to lead children from one state to the other. The Bullock Report[2] tackled this problem in the chapter 'Language and Learning', suggesting that to 'bring knowledge into being is a formulating process, and language is its ordinary means'. The Report continued: 'What is known must in fact be brought to life afresh with every "knower" by his own efforts'.

The child's approach to information is not, of course, the same as the adult's. Before we set about buying resources we should recognize two particularly important differences. These are the young child's use of fantasy as a means of learning, and his difficulty in dealing with the abstract.

The habit of phasing in and out of fantasy was noted by Piaget[3], and reported in rather disapproving tones. When Piaget questioned children about the natural world, he was frequently puzzled by their answers. These were often not only untrue, but known to be untrue by the children. Piaget called this response 'romancing', and concluded that children may 'invent an answer simply because they like the sound of it'. The Rosens[4] corroborate Piaget's findings, citing written work in which fantasy and factual elements intertwine. For example, a description of a caterpillar has a little digression: 'It is trying to read my name'. A study of triangles moves into an account of making 'Flying Saucer Mark 100 from the year 2020'. This sliding from what Susan Isaacs[5] called 'reality-thinking' to fantasy may be an indication of an intellectual stage, or simply an ignorance of adult conventions. It may also be a protective device, a way of cutting off when the information given by adults is inappropriate or unacceptable. Kornei Chukovsky[1] believes that the child is 'armored against thoughts and information that he does not need, and that are prematurely offered to him by too-hasty adults'. He quotes as example the child of five who was told by his mother how babies were born, and began at once to improvise a story about a little house inside the mother's tummy. He was turning away from information for which he was not ready.

Piaget and other observers have noted the inability of young children to deal with the abstract. This finding has an important implication for the way in which we present information. Children's language begins with the personal and then moves to the impersonal, and their approach to information shows a similar pattern, developing from the anecdotal to the formulation of hypotheses. As Marjorie

Hourd[6] explains: 'The ideal of a knowledge embodied in strictly impersonal statements now appears contradictory' – a view upheld by the Bullock Report. We process or interpret information through creating our own links between what is new and what is familiar. Before new knowledge can be brought into use it has to be integrated with our existing store. Adults develop techniques for dealing efficiently with new facts. Young children deal with information most easily when it has a personal slant.

Both these points should be borne in mind when choosing non-fiction for the First School age-group. The child's curiosity is an asset on which we should capitalize, through appropriate teaching programmes and the provision of a wide range of information resources. These resources need to be chosen with an eye to children's developmental characteristics, as well as to standard book selection criteria.

The books available

The term 'non-fiction' probably conjures up a picture of a traditional information book, setting out to present facts about a specific subject. There is a long history of publications of this kind, from the nineteenth-century works of Peter Parley, through the closely-packed Methuen *Outlines* and Bodley Head *Study Books* of a quarter century ago, to current series such as Black's *Junior Reference Books*, Blackwell's *Learning Library* or Hamish Hamilton's *Small World*. However, the non-fiction category now embraces a wide range of purposes. As our understanding of children's learning processes has deepened, so publishers have sought to find books which fit these new perceptions.

Perhaps most appropriate to the needs of young children are the books one can call 'induction aids'. These are simple introductions to everyday life, designed to help children understand their immediate environment. There is a potential classification problem here. Some stories have such a realistic background that they can count as little quasi-documentaries, while some information books are presented in such a personalized way that they seem little different from stories. Books in this category may portray family or school situations, or they may try to encourage particular attitudes, such as tolerance of different life styles, conservation of natural resources, or understanding of handicap.

Then there are the non-fiction books which are more concerned to communicate experience than tell facts. What is it like to be a fisherman, or a fireman? What would we see or feel on a journey down a river, on a mainline train, or at the seaside? (A good example of the genre at adult level is Lawrence Durrell's *The Greek Islands* (Faber) which gives something beyond facts – a sense of place.) This group of books is obviously important in the light of suggestions that information makes more impact when presented in a personal way. The personal slant engages children's interest and helps them relate the information to what they already know.

We are also now more aware that children learn through their own discoveries. Some publications take this principle as their base, and specifically set out to stimulate curiosity and motivate children to test assumptions, make observations etc. These are the books which encourage children's own thinking – and anyone who has read *Primary Education in England*[7] will have noted the importance put on the development of thought by Her Majesty's Inspectorate. Their survey recommended a greater depth in the curriculum, and the encouragement of speculation and observation. One hopes for an increasing number of books to help teachers to work in this way. Science, history and social studies are areas particularly suited to this approach.

All schools need some practical handbooks. These link with direct experience in a slightly different way. They aim to improve techniques and to increase creativity, and are usually concerned with crafts and hobbies.

Even young children need access to precise factual information at times, a role filled by quick-reference books. In this group come dictionaries, encyclopedias, atlases, and similar works designed to give fairly brief answers to specific questions. It is unfortunate that little quick-reference material is produced just for First School readership. In the circumstances teachers and librarians have to make use of books intended for older age-groups. For example, in identifying birds, the best source is likely to be an adult guide such as the *Oxford Book of Birds* or Collins' *Field Guide to the Birds of Britain and Europe.* It is in this area that the selection of stock is most likely to be a compromise between children's capacity and publishers' offerings.

The non-fiction field has expanded greatly in the last few years, as publishers have responded to changes in teaching methods. The Secondary and Middle Schools are better served than the Junior and First Schools, but the range of stock for younger children has improved in the face of representation from librarians and educationists. One positive impetus has come from the establishment of a Junior Information Book Award by *The Times Educational Supplement.* However, teachers and librarians still complain that publishers do not pay enough attention to the lower end of the age scale. The problem is not so much a lack of books, as a lack of those showing an understanding of young children's limitations and teachers' aims.

It was about a decade ago that the problem was first voiced in the educational press. A spate of books designed for First Schools followed these articles. They were characterized by a short text, simple sentence structures, and strong visual appeal. Among pioneer series were Brockhampton's Picture Science Books, Hamish Hamilton Star

Books, and Macdonald Educational's Starters. Several of the series launched at this time are now either discontinued or out of print. There are a variety of reasons for this. Some editors were more concerned with sales figures than content. The books they produced looked attractive and sold quickly, but proved, on closer examination, to be inaccurate or poorly organized. Such series ceased because they no longer commanded teachers' confidence. Other books, well received in their time, became dated in appearance as taste in page layout and illustration changed. We could benefit from a new publishing initiative, taking into account recent insights into the process of knowledge acquisition, the concept level of young children, and new views of the topic method. It is unfortunate that, although non-fiction books represent a large proportion of sales, fiction and picture books remain the prestige areas in children's publishing.

When information books are being discussed, staff needs are often forgotten. However, we should be building book resources to service the needs of the whole school community. Therefore, in considering the many categories of stock needed, we must remember to include reference works and books on curricular areas for the use of staff as well as children.

Making a choice

We can choose wisely only if we know the purpose behind our choices. Here we are back to the need for working out a school book policy which sets out the purposes served by book resources. Similarly, we cannot choose wisely unless we know the range of material available. By choosing just from the information books in the local bookshop, or just from the publishers' catalogues which land on our desk, we are limiting the educational opportunities of our children. Yet, so often, this is what happens. No wonder that the National Book League report, *Books for Schools*[8], deplores the haphazard way in which school books are chosen, and recommends a system to provide much clearer guidance to teachers on new publications.

It is obviously advantageous to see books before ordering them. It would be unreasonable to expect small local shops to have a comprehensive range on their shelves, but the local Education Library Service certainly should be able to help. The majority of those in English counties have exhibition collections of new and standard publications, which teachers can examine at their leisure. Nearly half the English county library systems run a purchase scheme, enabling schools to buy direct from Education Library stock. The Library Association can provide more information on these schemes, while your local library or Education Department will be able to tell you if they are in operation in your area.

Choosing non-fiction stock is a two-stage process. First we have to decide on the quality of the particular book we are assessing. Second, we have to decide whether it is more or less suitable than other titles on the subject. The second step does require access to a large exhibition stock, or to workshop collections. The first is basically the job any critic or reviewer has to do. Here are some of the points to take into consideration.

Purpose

The first task is to decide the book's purpose. What is the author setting out to do? For example, a book on birds may be an identification guide; it may be anecdotal; it may describe habits and behaviour, or it may offer practical advice on bird-watching, making bird tables, feeding in winter etc. The selector must see that the purpose of the book matches the library's needs. Clues to purpose may be given on the book-jacket or title page, or in the preface. It is strange that currently only a minority of books give this basic information, although the need for some kind of introduction is obvious.

Subject coverage

Accuracy is the factor which gets most publicity when non-fiction is being discussed, but inaccuracies are relatively rare among publishers of repute. A high proportion of information books are team compilations, or are supervised by a panel of experts; with such a production pattern, mistakes should be few. No one teacher or librarian is likely to have enough knowledge to be able to spot inaccuracies over the whole subject-range, but, within a school or library staff, it is probable that a range of expertise can be found to check dubious sections. What one may have to question more is the degree to which complex material can be simplified. There is a point at which such a process becomes counter-productive. Some subjects, for example historical issues or scientific concepts, are not within the understanding of young children, and attempts at summarizing merely leads to distortion or misrepresentation. Publishers occasionally make the mistake of equating brevity with simplicity. For example, in *Whales* (Macdonald Educational: Starters series) we have a two-sentence attempt to explain the animal's breathing system. 'A whale has to come up for air. This makes a spout.' Children require a more detailed treatment than this. Basically, we have to decide whether the coverage given to the subject is appropriate. Is it too cursory, or is it too detailed? Is it relevant to the interests of the likely audience? Are some aspects given insufficient attention? Some of these questions may be resolved only by reference to comparable publications.

Organization

A book intended for information retrieval should be designed to make the task easy. This means an uncrowded contents page with clear headings, and an index with entries that lead to information worth having. (Do check a sample.) It also means a logical arrangement of content. Examination of a group of books on the same subject will usually help you to assess suitable arrangement of material. In some cases the order of content is almost dictated by the subject. It is sensible to progress through the life cycle of an animal, through the seasons on the farm, through a chronological sequence in history. Children move in understanding from the particular to the general, and some authors take account of this characteristic. *The Airline Pilot* (Macmillan) begins with Captain Porter opening the engines on his Trident Three, and then moves out to information on airports, flight control, types of aircraft. *Forester* (Nelson) starts with a description of David Owen's home in the Welsh mountains, and only gradually brings in details of his work as a forester. Occasionally an author tries to arouse interest by taking the reader by surprise. *Down the River* (Puffin), for example, opens with two children spilling a glass of water, and so making a short river. The author then lists the longest rivers in the world before describing river formation.

An arresting opening section is fine, but we must always read beyond, to make sure that the rest of the book lives up to this promise. Too many books for young children are simply collections of facts, without any sense of development of argument or viewpoint. In any book claiming to deal with subject knowledge, this must be judged a defect. There should be some concluding section, pulling together the information offered or helping the reader judge its significance. Sometimes a text is organized on a two-stage basis, so that younger children can read the picture captions or a brief description, and fluent readers can proceed to more detailed information. This is a helpful device, extending potential readership. Examples of the technique can be seen in the Easy Reading editions of Macdonald Educational's Visual Books, and in the Nature's Way series produced by G. Whizzard/Andre Deutsch. Another aid to readers is a list of additional sources of information. This is a regular bonus in Black's Junior Reference Books, and a feature of some series from Macdonald Educational. Unfortunately, it is a feature neglected by the majority of publishers.

Design and illustration

Children expect books to have a high standard of visual appeal, and are unlikely to turn to those which fail in this respect. There are many factors for adults to check here. The book should look as if thought has been given to its overall design. For a First School readership the print size should be large enough for letter shapes to be clearly distinguished, lines should be fairly short, and not set too close together. As we saw in Chapter Three, illustrations can either decorate or extend a text. Initially we should try to establish what purpose the illustrations are trying to fulfil, and how suitable they are for this role. In most non-fiction books illustrations provide essential information difficult to express in words – the sheen of a dragonfly's wing, the plan of a castle, the machinery of a lock. We need to check their level of success as carriers of visual messages. Clearly, to be effective, illustrations should be near the relevant text and in a form which First School pupils will understand.

Just as the text of an information book can provide an imaginative experience, so can its illustrations. Many different techniques can achieve such an effect. See, for example, the striking photographs, with unusual detail, in Joe Van Wormer's *Elephants* (Angus & Robertson), the use of children's drawings in Zaidee Lindsay's *West Indies* (Black), or Juliette Palmer's evocative colour work in *Swanupping* (Macmillan).

Sense of audience

Audience rapport is perhaps the most important feature of nonfiction. We learn from Wolfgang Iser that reading is an active engagement with text, but far too few authors realize that their first aim must be to facilitate this meeting of child and book. Almost any batch of new publications will afford examples of ways in which authors keep their readers at arms length. We find the abstract or scholarly text, the condescending tone, the text which oppresses the reader by its weight of facts. How different is the arresting opening of *How Big is Big?* (Hodder) – 'Your hand is made of more atoms than there are leaves on all the trees . . .' – or of *Sciurus: The Story of a Grey Squirrel* (Collins): 'Sciurus woke with a start; something strange had given him a fright . . .'.

Any author needs to gain the confidence and interest of his reader. Writers addressing themselves to children should be especially aware of this obligation. The less fluent the reader, the more he requires assurance that reading the book will be rewarding. Such assurance comes partly from the teacher, but partly from the author's tone and presentation of the information. Children like to get the feeling of a personal voice telling them something new and interesting.

The research of Lunzer and Gardner[9] shows that Secondary School pupils take in information more readily if it is presented in a personal way. This must apply even more in the First School. Teachers and librarians should take such characteristics into account when assessing new books. To reach a decision it is essential to read continuous passages of text, and try to react to them in terms of children's understanding. Browsing through the text is no use. Any day one can see teachers and librarians selecting books by flicking through the pages – a method which can give only a general impression. Bright pictures may motivate a child to begin reading, but only an impelling text can keep him reading.

The potential of project work

From infant to secondary level we can find teachers busy with what is variously described as project work, topic work, or resource based learning. Basically, it is subject work with a strong element of flexibility in the organization. It requires active participation by the pupils, and support from a range of books and other resources. As Robert Hoare[10] puts it: 'Topic work may be summarised as extended work on a selected theme, generally taking in a variety of subjects in the traditional curriculum, but occasionally confined to one. In topic work, the children work individually or in groups under the direction of the teacher, collecting, collating, and recording information obtained from first-hand observation or by reference books'.

As with so many other aspects of education, there is evidence of great activity and little questioning. In view of the large amount of time spent on topic work, it is particularly surprising that so little has been written of its purpose and methods. There is a strong case for some reference to topic work being included in the school book policy. Each school will want to reach its own conclusions. The following comments are designed to set out some of the issues and alternative approaches which merit discussion.

Aims

One can think of the aims of project work either in terms of the school curriculum or in terms of the pupil.

For those who favour the former, a helpful starting point is the survey, *Primary Education in England*. Here, in Annex B, are listed the factors referred to by Her Majesty's Inspectorate in their observation of classes. They amount, in effect, to a checklist of important elements in each area of the curriculum. They can serve as guidelines to schools seeking to compile programmes of work. Some such framework is essential if children's time is to be used to the best advantage, and same sense of academic progression achieved as they move up the school. The survey makes it clear that work programmes are rarely in evidence, so that children repeat the same subjects, or make little progression in subject knowledge. The comments on geography teaching illustrate the point. 'The 7 year olds learned about the immediate environment and more distant places to the same extent. Similar topics, for example, "homes" or "life on the farm" or "children of other lands" tended to appear in classes of all ages.'

One of the problems about seeing subject knowledge as the aim of project work is the large area of disagreement on curriculum content in First Schools. Is there a body of knowledge which children should have acquired by the time they are eight? If so, what does it consist of, and on what basis do we make choices? Vikings or Victorians, Prehistory or Local history, Plants or Planets – which should we choose? Under current conditions it is quite possible for children to have 'done' the same subject three times within the same school. 'Oh, not dinosaurs again!' 'We did the Post Office last year, miss.' When there is so much that young children need to know, it is disturbing that their time and enthusiasm can be wasted by this lack of liaison. The message must be firmer planning and greater coordination of subject work within the school.

When Vincent Rogers[11], an American, investigated attitudes to topic work in British Primary Schools, he found teachers were more concerned with process than product, with how a child learns rather than what he learns. If his findings are correct, we must assume that for most teachers the purpose of project work is acquisition of skills and attitudes rather than information. Given such an aim, it is obviously desirable that schools should itemize these learning skills. Where no school documentation exists, each teacher will be faced with building up some objectives, if only to assure herself of some progress.

Support and help for individual teachers can come from workshops and study groups. In Berkshire, for example, there are opportunities each year for in-service sessions on information book use and study skills. Wiltshire now builds into reading courses some sessions on information books, and other authorities are showing an increased interest in the subject. How much individual children will be able to achieve will, of course, vary, but the skills to be considered include:

identifying suitable sources (e.g. which book to consult);
locating appropriate information within a book;
comparing versions of the same event;
summarizing the information found;
deciding the significance of the information.

Some First Schools will look at topic work from quite a different angle. Instead of being concerned with facts to be learnt or skills to be acquired, they will see this kind of work as an agency of personal development. It will be regarded as a way of stimulating curiosity, of demonstrating that learning is enjoyable, of enabling children to progress at their own pace. In such schools, teachers will claim that topic work encourages positive attitudes to school work and also enriches children's own experience. Depending on the way it is organized, it can foster collaboration or give children a chance to work independently.

It is necessary to analyse aims in some detail, so that work has the right direction. Many schools will decide that project work should achieve all the major objectives noted here. With thought, that is quite possible. The Primary School survey confirms that 'the range of work and the standards achieved are interrelated, sometimes in ways that are not immediately obvious'. It warns that 'a narrow concentration on teaching a skill is not always the best way of achieving high standards in it.' With careful planning, the skills can be taught and attitudes formed, within the context of subject interest.

Starting points

Sometimes a topic will be undertaken as part of a planned programme of subject work, on the lines suggested in *Primary Education in England*. At other times it may arise from a national or local event – a major exhibition, a school jubilee, the start of a new bypass or housing development. The interest could develop from a story shared or from one child's family news.

Whatever the initial impetus, the teacher has a role in guiding and shaping the project. Although we often think of project work as something quite distinct from language work, in fact it offers great opportunities for the development of all language skills. One can begin by getting the children to talk about the project. What aspects of the subject could be considered? What do they know already? What would it be interesting to find out? Before the children begin any reading or writing we want them to begin thinking. Of course, the younger the children, the more adult guidance they will need, but often they will surprise us by their perception. Again, the Primary School survey is relevant. It urges teachers to raise their assumptions of what children are capable of doing, and to 'establish sequences of learning in all subjects which will enable children to . . . have confidence in their own abilities and capacities.'

One of the most important decisions for the teacher is how to frame the project. If topic work becomes largely an exercise in copying, the fault probably lies in the way the project was presented. A blanket instruction, such as 'Find out about butterflies', gives little direction to children, and their quite sensible response is to find a book on the subject and copy out what seem to be the appropriate parts. A better beginning is to form with the children a series of questions to be answered or problems to be solved. 'Do wasps do any good?' 'Was a castle a comfortable place to live?' 'What traces of the Romans can you find in our town?' With this kind of approach answers cannot be discovered by reading only. The child has to think over what he has read, add to it from his existing knowledge, and reach fresh conclusions. Piaget spoke of education as 'the deliberate cultivation of the ability to think'. There is no reason why, even in the First School, we should not be offering planned opportunities for the development of thought.

Working methods

Discussion of the topic and gathering of relevant books can take place simultaneously. At this stage both the resources available and the ideas coming forward will influence the form of the study. Gradually the outline of the topic will be built up. Hoare's *Topic work with books*, although a little dated, is useful in setting out different strategies, but, in practice, each teacher will develop his or her own working methods. All of us can benefit from the experience of colleagues, and should seek opportunities for discussing project organization with them. Here are some hints drafted by a Berkshire study group on this subject.

1 Whatever the subject content of the project, be clear about the learning skills you want the children to acquire or practise.
2 Don't organize every topic in the same way. This only bores you and the class, apart from being very limiting.
3 Recognize both the convenience and value of group work. It is easier to monitor the progress of six groups of five children than to watch over thirty individual studies. The group structure encourages exploration of the theme, and lets us make use of the particular gifts of individual children.
4 Bear in mind the value of topic work in taking us over subject boundaries.
5 Remember the role of fiction and poetry in giving an extra dimension to subject work.
6 Make a place for direct experience and observation wherever possible.
7 Use audio-visual materials as well as books wherever appropriate.
8 Keep a brief note of each project undertaken, including useful books. If these are filed centrally they will help you and other colleagues.

Resources are an integral part of any project. The first step is to check what the school has – and this implies a well-arranged central book collection. The second is to check outside sources, such as the Education Library service, the local Teachers' Centre, and the Museum service.

At an early stage the teacher will decide how the results of the topic are to be presented. There may be written work, co-operative folders, art work, drama, tapes, an exhibition or wall display. Here again, we should look for variety of approach. Teachers often ask how long a topic should last. It is sensible to keep the timing flexible. Nothing is worse than announcing a four-week project, and then being unable to sustain interest. With young children, concentration and interest are usually better if the project takes place in a fairly short span of time.

Some educationists believe that too much time is given in schools today to the use of information books, at the expense of literature. Walker[12] makes this point in *Reading Development and Extension*. However, he is attacking not information itself, but our treatment of it. It would be a pity to deny opportunities for children's natural zest for knowledge to find expression. Given the will and imagination, we can devise programmes which are flexible, which stimulate rather than blunt curiosity. We can take confidence from the great interest in factual books shown by children. Whitehead's survey[13], admittedly of the 10+ group, found that 25% of recreational reading among the 10+ group lay in this area. Margaret Clark[14], in her study of young children, reported great enjoyment of non-fiction, especially among boys. Often the way-in with poor readers is through their subject interests, but, as Gray and Rogers[15] report, subject interest is also a strong motivator for fluent readers. Finding the facts is a pursuit children enjoy; only unimaginative teaching makes it dull.

The reference collection

In the strict sense of the term, all the non-fiction books can be described as reference material, because we refer to them for information. However, when we talk of 'reference books' in connection with a school or library, we usually mean something much more specific. In this sense, reference books are those designed for quick reference rather than continuous reading. In most cases they are shelved in a separate section of the library (or classroom), and are not allowed to be borrowed for home reading.

This collection is often the most hard-worked section of the library, available at all times to answer enquiries. It is easy, though, to waste a great deal of money on reference books. Before you buy, work out exactly what you hope your reference collection will do. Here are a few points to bear in mind.

1 No library can be self-contained. Even the reference stock of a large city library will not be sufficient to answer every question received. Buy your stock taking into account the other libraries you can call on for information.

2 Recognize that reference books get out of date. Your budget should

take into account the need to replace stock at intervals by new editions or new titles.

3 Do not be pressurized by salesmen into making instant decisions. Examine rival publications and consult with colleagues. Give yourself time to make the right choice.

4 Few quick-reference books are designed just for First Schools. Therefore, selection is particularly difficult, and your final choice is almost bound to be a compromise.

5 Staff need sources of information as well as children. Allow for this in your budget.

6 Do not buy reference books just for the sake of having an impressive section. Always relate your purchases to the range of questions you are likely to receive.

7 Remember that your real objective is not book provision, but book use. It is therefore important to design school programmes which involve recourse to reference books.

Precisely which reference books to buy is a matter for each school or library to decide, in the light of its readers and its work patterns. In the Workshop section of this chapter, examples of various categories of reference book are described. Practical work on these titles will help teachers build up criteria for making appropriate choices.

References

1. Chukovsky, K. *From Two to Five.* Berkeley, University of California Press: Cambridge University Press, 1968.
2. Department of Education & Science. *A Language for Life.* (The Bullock Report) HMSO, 1975.
3. Piaget, J. *The Child's Conception of the World.* Routledge, 1929.
4. Rosen, C. & H. *The Language of Primary School Children.* Penguin Education, 1973.
5. Isaacs, S. *The Intellectual Growth of Young Children.* Routledge, 1930.
6. Hourd, M. *Relationships in Learning.* Heinemann Educational, 1972.
7. Department of Education & Science. *Primary Education in England.* HMSO, 1978.
8. National Book League. *Books for Schools.* National Book League, 1979.
9. Lunzer, E. & Gardner, K. *The Effective Use of Reading.* Heinemann Educational, 1979.
10. Hoare, R. *Topic Work with Books.* Geoffrey Chapman, 1971.
11. Rogers, V. 'English and American Primary Schools.' In Sebesta, S.L. & Wallen, C.J. *The First R.* Chicago, Science Research Associates, 1972.
12. Walker, C. *Reading Development and Extension.* Ward Lock Educational, 1974.
13. Whitehead, F. *and others. Children and their Books.* Macmillan, 1977.
14. Clark, M. *Young Fluent Readers.* Heinemann Educational, 1976.
15. Gray, W.S. & Rogers, B. *Maturity in Reading.* Chicago, University of Chicago Press, 1956.

Booklist

Within the scope of this guide, it is not possible to list every non-fiction book which might have a use for First School pupils. In any case, book lists date quickly and are not an effective way of choosing books. The lists below indicate the range of material available in a few subject areas, and introduce some popular series. The books included could be brought together for workshops on book selection or project work. However you use the lists, do remember that series-publishing is mainly a means of keeping down production costs. No series consists of books of equal quality, so each title requires individual assessment.

Transport

Transporting Goods, by K.S. Allen. Franklin Watts (A First Look Book)
A historical account, illustrated by line drawings. The information is clear and interesting, but no attempt is made to do more than present facts. Makes use of a device common to all First Look Books – bold type for certain key words. This is acceptable for specialized vocabulary (eg 'sledge', 'submarines'), but hard to justify for 'animals', 'feet', and similar everyday words. Has an index but no contents page.
Going on a Train, by Althea. Dinosaur Publications (Althea Series: Blue Label)
Stolid coloured illustrations and approachable text working together to introduce the railway system. No index, no contents page.
Land Travel, edited by R. Canter. Macmillan. (Look It Up series)
Well organized information, with striking illustrations and good page layout. Suitable for a wide age-range. The text is mainly confined to factual information, but there is some attempt to provoke thought.
Early Railways, by Henry Cummings. Macdonald Educational (Toppers series)
An example of a book not designed specifically for First Schools, but useful for background information. A well organized work, with attractive layout, and suggestions for local observation.
Keith and Sally Out and About, by Alain Grée. Evans (Keith and Sally series)
Information presented through the narrative mode. Keith and Sally, tireless learners, try to find the most suitable way of sending a kitten to their uncle. The attempt involves (perhaps rather tediously) almost every form of transport. Some craft activities and word lists are included. Jolly characters and bright cereal-packet illustrations.
My Big Book of Cars, Ships and Planes. Macdonald Educational
A wide-ranging survey, with clever page layout. Each double-spread has one large picture, with caption in large type; surrounding this are smaller pictures and text, giving supplementary information for more fluent readers. Far from a quality product, but likely to be a popular

browsing book. Macdonald Educational have a habit of using the same material in many forms, without making this clear to the purchaser. This book is, in fact, an amalgam of several titles in the Beginner's World series. (See, for example, *Cars, Lorries and Trains* in that series.)

Let's Go to the Railway Station, by F. Peacock. Franklin Watts. ('Let's go' series)

A book with similar aims to Althea's *Going on a Train*, but using very different techniques. The illustrations are coloured photographs, the text is shorter, the type face larger. The words relating to railways are printed in bold type, and also set out separately in a vocabulary check-list.

The Airline Pilot, by C. Rayman. Macmillan Education (What Do They Do series)

A painless introduction to air transport, as we follow the working day of an aircraft pilot. Clear text and photographs.

Science

Household Machines, by Althea Braithwaite. Puffin Books (New Puffin Picture Book)

A firm family setting for an explanation of the working of all the machines the Fords need throughout the day. The diagrams are an essential feature, supplementing the information in the text.

Push, Pull: Empty, Full, by T. Hoban. Kestrel.

Engaging black and white photographs to demonstrate fifteen pairs of opposites. The skilful teacher can use this work as a starting point for discussion, bringing in more advanced books as appropriate.

Red, by Felicia Law. Collins (Dandelions series)

The aim of this series is to 'encourage children to use all their talents – practical and imaginative – in a new, integrated way'. Here the author explores many aspects of the term 'red' – scientific, historical, proverbial. Much of the book contains suggestions for experiments and craft work the children can undertake.

Weather, edited by A. Sheehan. Macdonald Educational (Macdonald First Library)

One of a series designed for the 6 – 8 age group, and leading on to more formal information books. Although the sentences are short and the vocabulary limited, many of the concepts are quite complex. Has an index but no contents page.

Things Up and Down, by Henry Pluckrose. Franklin Watts.

Black and white photographs and a brief text introduce some basic spatial concepts. The author tries to encourage reader participation.

Sounds, by A.P. Sanday. Ladybird Books. (Ladybird Leaders series)

One of a series designed with inexperienced readers in mind. Vocabulary is controlled, the type face large, the illustrations clear. The information is presented in such a way that enquiry and experiment are encouraged.

Under the Sea, by Brenda Thompson. Sidgwick & Jackson. (First Facts series)

An information book designed by a reading specialist, with the aim of making 'first steps in learning and reading an exciting adventure'. Bright coloured pictures and very brief text: short on hard facts.

A Wrigley Book About Time, by Denis Wrigley. Lutterworth (Wrigley Books)

A brave attempt to help children understand the complexities of time. Humorous line drawings and a text to stimulate further discussion.

The natural world

Frogs, by Althea. Longman (Life-Cycle Books)

Specially designed for young children, with bright, uncluttered illustrations and a short text set in large type.

Life on the Seashore, by H. Angel. Macmillan Education (Fact Finders series)

A modest paperback series, with well-arranged information and stimulating illustrations. Has a good index and a useful glossary.

Hedgehogs, by Oliver Aston. Basil Blackwell (Wild Life Studies)

Noticeable more for its attractive coloured photographs than for its organization. No contents page and no index for this episodic account of hedgehog habits.

Common Frog, by George Bernard. G. Whizzard. (Nature's Way series)

Outstanding colour plates and brief text, plus an introduction giving additional explanation. Received the *Times Educational Supplement* Junior Information Book Award.

Animal Camouflage, by J. Carthy. Bodley Head (Natural Science Picture Books)

Explores some of the ways in which animals protect themselves by making themselves less visible. Much praised on its publication in 1972. The layout and unbroken sections of text now look a little dated – an indication of the way information presentation has changed in the intervening years.

Field Animals, by F. Hall. Puffin Books (New Puffin Picture Book)

A description of the many birds, insects and animals to be found in a typical field, enhanced by softly coloured illustrations. No index or contents page.

Exploring the Park, by L. Jackman. Evans (Exploring Books)

A book designed to stimulate observation, practical work and questioning. The meticulous camera work of Leslie Jackman draws attention to significant and interesting aspects of the wild life of parkland.

Nature Fun, by J. Mellanby. Transworld (Wonder Why Books)
There is a serious intent behind the comic pictures which make this book so approachable. The emphasis throughout is on activities, which range from collecting woodlice and setting up a wormery to taking bark rubbings and making a nature trail.

History

Houses and Homes, by C. Bowyer. Usborne
A survey of houses in other times and other countries. Much of the book is in the picture-strip form characteristic of the Usborne production style. An amazing amount of information is contained, although some is so condensed as to be misleading. Usborne could be said to have developed the pictorial information book from the initial work of Macdonald Educational.

Cooks and Kitchens. Macdonald Educational. (Starters Long Ago Books)
Displays both the strengths and weaknesses of this series. The organization of material is poor, the text over-simplified, the time clues insufficient. On the credit side the illustrations are spirited, the format encouraging.

Homes, by D. Eddershaw. Nelson (Highways & Byways series)
A study of two Victorian families which seeks reader participation through direct questions and suggestions for activities. Uses the technique of a two-level text, so that fluent readers can proceed to more detailed information. Although a modest publication, it does include a list of other books on the subject.

Across the Mountains, by S. Howell. Macdonald Educational (Macdonald Adventures)
The life story of Gladys Aylward's mission to China, told in simple language. Suitable for a wide age-range.

Roman Britain, by P. Sauvain. Macmillan Education (Imagining the Past series)
The series title, 'Imagining the Past', indicates the approach. Philip Sauvain works to help us recreate the past and imagine what life was like 1,700 years ago. Photographs of Roman relics supplement the evocative line drawings.

This is essentially a stimulus book, and can be used in a variety of ways with a variety of audiences.

In History: Schools, by D. Smith & D. Newton. Schofield & Sims. (In History series)
The Primary School experience of the authors helps them achieve an interesting and informal approach. There are attractive coloured

illustrations on each page, and a fairly brief text which teachers will probably need to supplement from other sources.
Two Victorian Families, by S. Wagstaff. Black.
An interesting example of a personal approach to history. This study of the servants and family of a Victorian household brings out clearly the different living standards of rich and poor. While not written for First Schools, the treatment makes the information easy to absorb. A teachers' kit is also available as a unit or in parts.
Symbols and Signs, by F. Wilkins. Basil Blackwell (Learning Library)
Again, it is interesting to compare this pioneer series with more recent ones where the pictorial element predominates. Although the text here is quite long, the style is reassuring and children are encouraged to relate the information given to their own surroundings.

Selection aids

There are no completely satisfactory bibliographies of information books for this age-group. One problem is that there are few specialists in this field. The other is the rapidity with which new titles are published and old ones go out of print – there are no classics in the non-fiction market.
    The most appropriate guide, being an annotated list of nearly one hundred and fifty titles, is:
Five to Eight, compiled by Janet Fisher. The Library Association, Youth Libraries Group.
A selection of about one hundred new non-fiction books for children is usually included in:
Children's Books of the Year. H. Hamilton in association with the National Book League.
Advice about basic stock or new publications can be sought from the Public Library service or the local Education library service, and the opinion of colleagues with specialist knowledge can be canvassed.
    A book which seeks to give its readers the critical apparatus to deal with any non-fiction book is:
Matters of Fact, by Margery Fisher. Brockhampton, 1972.
Here Margery Fisher takes a number of subjects – e.g. Bread, The Postal System, Cowboys, Time – and surveys the books available, analysing their approach, assessing their success. An unannotated booklist is appended to each chapter. Although the coverage is not limited to First School readership, the critical techniques introduced can be applied to any level or subject. The text really needs to be accompanied by the books discussed, and the book may therefore be of most value in workshop sessions.
    Each year since 1973 *The Times Educational Supplement* has offered a Junior Information Book Award. The comments of the judges

usually appear in the last October or first November issue, and are useful in the building up of criteria for selection in this field.

Workshop comparisons

General knowledge

General knowledge books do not cover the wide range of subjects which an encyclopedia should, but they have a value in attracting children to reference books, and in providing useful background information. They are usually single-volume works, with plenty of illustrations. Arrangement is usually thematic rather than alphabetical. Misleadingly, many of these general knowledge books are called 'encyclopedia', but a little reflection will make one realize that the kind of comprehensive coverage an encyclopedia attempts is unlikely to be achieved by a single volume costing £5 or so.

Examples

Boys' and girls' encyclopedia, by Jean Stroud. Hamlyn, 1973.
Twenty-eight articles of two to four pages, arranged in a roughly developmental sequence, beginning with The Universe, and moving through Prehistory to the natural world and then on to machines. Consider particularly the organization of information within articles – see, for example, Pets or Sports. The main concession to young children is the general use of short sentences, with simple structures, and the range of subjects covered – most of the content is relevant to First School interests. Illustrations are clear and plentiful, albeit undistinguished.
Look and Find Out Encyclopedia, by R.J. Unstead. Collins, 1972.
An imaginative attempt to present pictorial information to young children. Most of the book consists of coloured double-spreads with, below, a brief description. At the back is a thirty page index for older children ('Look and find out A–Z'), cross-referenced to the pictures.
The Junior Encyclopedia of General Knowledge, eds T.R. Entwistle & J. Cooke. Octopus Books, 1978.
A handsome volume, generously illustrated by coloured photographs of high quality. It is arranged in eleven subject sections, subdivided into two-page articles. Designed for 8–12 year olds, and therefore largely beyond First School children. Interesting as an example of the genre; some potential value for teachers.

Encyclopedias

The early compilers of encyclopedias set out to include all knowledge within their pages. This aim has become increasingly unattainable as man's knowledge has widened. To a large extent, an encyclopedia nowadays serves as a first point of enquiry, leading us to more detailed sources of information. At First School level an encyclopedia can give only a very selective coverage of knowledge; our concern is to see that the contents match First School interests.

My First Colour Encyclopedia, by J.W. Watson. Hamlyn, 1970.

Rather like an extended picture dictionary, with 400 entries, fairly simple text and engaging colour work. One of the few reference works designed specifically for the First School age-group.

Black's Children's Encyclopaedia, eds W. Worthy & R.J. Unstead. Black, 1971. 2 vols.

One of the best-known children's encyclopedias, now in its third edition. Planned for the 8–12 age group. Looking a little dated now in its style of illustration, but still representing good value in terms of the range of information included and its sensible, clear presentation. Available also in a 12-part edition.

Our World Encyclopedia, edited by L. Sealey. Macmillan Education, 1975. 10 vols.

Departs from the traditional alphabetical order to a subject arrangement, each volume being given to a different topic. Well illustrated, interesting layout and thoughtful text. Designed for the Junior School market, but some of the content has an application in First Schools.

Dictionaries

Judging by the number in print, publishers are united on the educational importance of dictionaries. Selection is difficult partly because of the wide range available. Most schools will require several dictionaries, with simpler ones in the classrooms and fuller ones in the central library area.

At First School level, the emphasis is on meaning, pronunciation and spelling of words; derivation is less important. Do check that the definitions or illustrative sentences really explain the word, and do it in terms that children will understand. Compare the way in which different publications deal with the same words. A clear type face and uncluttered page are desirable features. Illustrations may be informative or merely decorative; check how useful they are. For younger children it is helpful if the letter forms used are similar to those the children use in their own writing.

Examples

Picture Dictionary, compiled by L. Derwent. Burke.

Described as a play book as well as a work book, this has an exceptionally attractive layout, with clear type face and bright illustrations. Includes the words most used by children of 5–8 years. The words are defined mainly through the use of illustrative sentences, a method which makes for interest rather than precision. Sometimes the enquirer is merely sent from one synonym to another, eg:

Afraid: When we are afraid we are full of fear.

Fear: When we are afraid we are full of fear.

The Oxford Junior Dictionary, compiled by R. Sansome. Oxford University Press.

Intended for children of 7–9 years, and contains approx. 5,000 words. Not illustrated, but has a very clear layout. The definitions are expressed in a basic vocabulary of 2,000 words, and are both exact and easy to understand. Illustrative sentences are provided wherever necessary.

One of a large range of Oxford dictionaries. At a much simpler level is *The Oxford Picture Word Book*, with 550 words. At a more advanced level is *The Oxford Children's Dictionary* (now distributed by Granada Publishing), with 11,000 entries. Examine for staff use the newly revised *Concise Oxford Dictionary*.

Chambers Young Set Dictionary, compiled by A. Brown and others. Chambers.

Four volumes, each a self-contained dictionary, but designed as a pack to span the changing needs.

Dictionary One: Designed for children of 4–5 years. No definitions, just a coloured picture to accompany each word.

Dictionary Two: Aimed at First School pupils. Clear but unremarkable layout, with black and white illustrations. Brief definitions and sometimes illustrative sentences. Some explanations are so simplified as to be misleading – see, for example, 'magazine' or 'passenger'.

Dictionary Three: Some overlap with the previous volume, with identical definitions. An informal style, employed with varying success.

Dictionary Four: Contains 15,000 words, and is intended for children of 10–11 years.

For staff use consider *Chambers Twentieth Century Dictionary*.

The Giant All-colour Dictionary, compiled by S. Courtis & G. Watters. Hamlyn.

A dictionary of American origin designed for children 7–11 years. Contains nearly 8,000 words, with full definitions and occasional illustrative sentences. Alternative meanings are set out clearly. Pronunciation is given wherever necessary; related parts of speech (eg plurals, past participles) are listed. Over 2,000 coloured illustrations, of limited use for identification, but adding to the book's attraction. An approachable book with good coverage.

Examine for staff use *Encyclopedic World Dictionary*, published by Hamlyn.

Atlases

Research has shown that even Secondary School pupils find difficulty in understanding maps. We must therefore not underestimate the perceptual and conceptual problems they pose for young children. While all atlases should cover the whole world, the emphasis for First Schools should be on the British Isles. When selecting, check that the atlas content is appropriate, and that the maps are clear and readable. Too much detail makes for an overcrowded map which is difficult to read.

Examples

Atlas One. Collins-Longman.
One of a recent series of four atlases, so graded and inter-related that they span all the school years. Most space in this initial volume is given to the British Isles. This attractive atlas has a clear introduction explaining its use: an accompanying work-book is available.
Philip's First Venture Atlas. George Philip.
An elementary atlas from a specialist publisher, reaching a high standard for clarity and colour. The small page size and large amount of marginal information are disadvantages.
The Hamlyn Boys' and Girls' Atlas. Hamlyn.
Interesting as an attempt to help children understand the shape and main features of the earth. Considerable use is made of pictorial symbols, which produces cluttered maps and a misleading impression. It would be easy to take away the view that England is full of merry Morris-men, and Spain occupied by dancing girls and bull-fighters, for example.

Consider for staff use *The Oxford School Atlas,* Collins-Longman's *Atlas Four* (designed for 'O' and 'A' level candidates), or Nelson's new *Atlas 80,* which has a range of unusual information and some pictorial sections. A vividly illustrated companion to geographical studies is *Planet Earth* (Purnell), which includes a 25 page atlas section.

Specific information

As well as the main categories of reference book, you are likely to need guides to help identify birds, plants, animals etc, and perhaps various forms of transport. Your choice will probably be between titles produced for the adult market, for example, the *Oxford Book of Flowers, Mammals of the World* (Methuen), *Oxford Book of Birds, Field Guide to the Birds of Britain and Europe* (Collins). Do remember to include in your reference section some local information, such as rail and bus timetables, a local map and street directory.

7

Organizing for use

Contents

The psychological environment
The physical environment
Patterns of organization
Stock

A book programme
References
Sources of help

The psychological environment

We must, of course, look for systems of organization which will ensure maximum use of resources bought for schools and libraries, in most cases at public expense. However, to begin with this as our organizational basis is to start from the wrong point. Our planning must start from a conviction that books are tools of education, and that we have a responsibility to give children opportunities to become familiar with them. By the time children leave the First School they should recognise books as sources of pleasure and information and have some facility in using them. Our aim should be to find an organization which promotes these purposes.

In this task the first consideration is the children themselves. They will come to school from widely differing backgrounds and, hence, with an infinite variety in the extent and quality of their experience. Some children will have known love and comfort, some will have a history of deprivation. Some will have a rich background of direct experience and a history of book use and book borrowing. Others will have no acquaintance with stories or picture books and no knowledge of the conventions of print. In *Young Fluent Readers*[1] Margaret Clark records the warmth of family relationships enjoyed by the high achieving children, while the National Children's Bureau document, *Born to Fail?*[2], is a sad reminder of family conditions for the 6% of British children who are disadvantaged. It is for both these extremes, as well as the majority who lie between, that we have to cater.

We can begin by educating ourselves about the stage the children have just passed through, making contacts with parents in the months before school entrance and with nearby nursery schools and play-groups. As we learn about the reading and viewing interests of under-fives, we can ensure that reception class children have access to familiar stories, filmstrips and pictures to help bridge the gap between their present and their past. As we learn about the attitudes towards school of under-fives, we can move to finding work and play program-mes in which they can feel comfortable. Margaret Clark has com-mented sharply on teachers' general disregard of the experience which children bring to school. It is a pity to waste the opportunities these experiences give by reacting to an 'average child' stereotype instead of welcoming and finding a place for individual differences. Provision of familiar books can be just one manifestation of a psychological environment of reassurance and security in which young children can flourish: as Creber[3] has stressed, we need to build up 'an atmosphere which is conducive to initiative, curiosity and participation'. The importance of the set, the collection of mental and emotional attitudes we bring to our work, is also emphasized by Aidan Chambers[4]. The presence of an interested adult who can give attention to children in an environment which is stimulating and encouraging has been shown by Clark to have a significant effect on children's achievement, and it is the ideal towards which we should work. If we can make the first encounters with books pleasurable, books will be regarded as a natural and enjoyable part of life. The importance of these early associations should not be undervalued: Joyce Morris's research[5] has shown both the influence of early reading experiences and the close relation between attitudes to reading and reading ability.

From our own adult learning experiences as well as our observation of children, we can see that success is a great motivator. Almost at once, unfortunately, some children are going to be faced with a sense of defeat as they come to the language and conventions of the world of books. This is a particularly acute problem for those not used to standard English. We have to go slowly, building on the language the children bring to school, and giving plenty of experience to listening to stories in standard English before moving on to the reading of stories from books. There is a difference of opinion about the extent to which teachers should seek to present non-standard English, and this is an issue to talk over with colleagues in the light of local circum-stances. Most children come to school in the expectation of learning and with some predisposition for change. We cannot change too much too quickly, and we should certainly not give children a feeling that they are rejected on grounds of their language. On the other hand, we have to recognize that the culture of the school is largely the culture of the book, and one of the teacher's major tasks is making children at home in that book world.

The physical environment

The young child's base is the classroom, and it is here that a high proportion of First School books will be found. Whatever the size or shape of the classroom, we need to create an area where children can look at books in comfort. This can be marked off by bookcases or seating acting as room dividers. It should have a domestic atmosphere, with carpet or rugs on the floor, curtains or pictures and informal seating, which may range from new rocking chairs and tub seats to donated settees and stools. A low table is useful to support books being consulted, for writing and for display.

The majority of books should be on display shelves, so that the front covers can be seen. Some horizontal shelving, on which books are stored with the spine only showing, will usually be needed as a supplement. Many specialist suppliers, such as Balmforth, Library Design & Engineering and Terrapin Reska, offer units which can be wall-hung or freestanding, carrying sloping and horizontal shelves or display panels, and with all shelves adjustable. Major public libraries can provide information on a range of suppliers and should be a source of advice on their products. The standard length of a bookshelf or case is 1 metre, and this length will accommodate about 40 children's books spine forwards, or about 10 if they are displayed with front cover showing. Obviously the height of shelving units should be related to pupil height: an overall height in the region of 1.3 to 1.5 metres is likely to be satisfactory. Shelf depth depends on the type of book to be stored, and it is sensible to measure some samples before reaching a decision. A depth of 20 cms will accommodate the majority of books. Cheaper shelving systems include Spur and Speedframe, and there is also plenty of scope for home-made or improvised shelving. Very simple display shelving can be constructed by attaching a shallow shelf about 7 cms deep on brackets to the wall, and fixing a lip about 4 cms deep to the front to keep the books in place. A very good source of ideas for people wanting to create book areas is Joan Dean's *Room to Learn: Language Areas*[6].

Some schools will have a central library area in addition to classroom space, and here one would hope to shelve at least one thousand books, so that the stock can be drawn on to give variety to class collections. The central library still needs an air of informality, but it will also be helpful to have one or two study tables and chairs associated with it for children wanting to make notes. A book trolley is a desirable accessory, and there should be some sections of pinboard and pegboard for display. With this larger collection some kind of shelf guiding will be required so that children can readily find what they need. Since the use of slides, tapes and filmstrips is usually linked with book use, it is probable that these materials will be best stored in the library area.

In deciding where to place books and other learning aids we need to recall purpose. We are trying to build up a reading environment which signals to children the interest and enjoyment residing in books and encourage them to sample this satisfaction. In such work, display will be a major aid. Display panels may be fixed to the wall, propped on tables or floor-mounted. They can be faced with softboard, hessian, wallpaper or polystyrene tiles. These panels may be used for notices, pictures, art work and children's writing, and can be associated with display tables, shelves or boards where books and objects can be placed. Joan Dean's *Room to Learn: Display*[7] contains many practical suggestions for using display techniques both to create quiet areas and to provide focal points.

Patterns of organization

In the past great arguments used to rage about the relative merits of classroom or central collections, but these have now largely been resolved. Any teacher will want some books at hand for immediate use, but no teacher can expect to have exclusive use of school resources. When stocks are limited some centralisation is an economy, for in this way each individual child is offered a wider choice. The basic point to remember is that books don't have to be fixed assets. If the central library is regarded as a pool from which teachers can draw and then return material, stock will be used to maximum effect, and classroom collections achieve variety and the ability to respond to special interests. The Bullock Report confirms the good sense of this two-level system, suggesting that the 'ebb and flow of books out of and into this [central] collection will be a continuous process' and emphasising the particular importance of achieving change of stock in vertically-grouped classrooms where children can be in the same environment for a considerable time.

The actual arrangement of books on the shelves depends a little on the geography of the school and the size of the book collection. In reaching a decision we have to ask why any arrangement system is necessary. With non-fiction the justification usually lies in the need to find information books on the same subject quickly, and staff are likely to want some simple subject classification for this purpose. Here it is advisable to find out whether any local decisions have been made. In Berkshire, for example, a standard colour coding is recommended for information books. This is based on the order of the Dewey Decimal classification (the scheme used in most British and American public libraries) and can incorporate a Dewey number. The full scheme is set out in Berkshire Education Department's *Reading Booklet No. 7* and the outline, showing its twelve colour base, is set out below. Other authorities may have similar schemes helpful in the First School.

Colour coding for information books

Colour	Subject	To include
Black	General knowledge	Encyclopedias, dictionaries, general knowledge books.
Silver	Religion	Bible stories, prayers, lives of saints and religious leaders. World religions.
Yellow	Social studies	The environment, social groups, people's jobs, government, law.
Brown	Transport	Transport by land, sea, air and in space.
Red	Science	General science, number, astronomy, physics and chemistry.
Dark green	Biology	Human beings, plants, animals, general nature study.
White	Technology	Industry, applied science, inventions.
Pale blue	Products	
Pink	The arts	Arts, crafts, sports and hobbies.
Pale green	Geography	Atlases, descriptions of other countries, people of other lands.
Dark blue	History and pre-history	Life in the past, castles, houses, costume through the ages.
Gold	Famous people	Biography, flags, heraldry.

It is also worthwhile to discuss the kind of arrangement needed for the rest of the stock, the stories, folk tales, poetry and picture books. Is any arrangement needed? Can it be maintained? Any system devised must be simple enough for the children to understand and operate. Many public libraries file stories alphabetically by author, but it may be better for the school to establish categories, e.g. picture books, supplementary readers, folk tales, or an arrangement by level of difficulty may be preferred. Cliff Moon offers guidance on classification into thirteen individualised reading stages, each colour-coded and shelved or boxed separately. Moon's booklet, *Individualised Reading*[8], sets out the advantages of the scheme and assists teachers in its application. The colour-coding of reading schemes, to enable teachers to correlate different stages in various schemes, is fairly widely accepted, but the arrangement of story books by reading level is a controversial issue. Opponents of this grading of library books say that it makes leisure reading just another school subject, that it overlooks the appeal of fiction – which is by reason of literary qualities and not vocabulary load, and, lastly, that it is extremely difficult to apply. Evidence from schools shows that either method can give good results, staff attitude being the crucial factor.

There is no doubt that children need guidance in choosing stories.

Our own observation of children is likely to persuade us of this, and the view has received confirmation recently in the research findings of the Schools Council project, 'Extending beginning reading'. The project leader, Vera Southgate-Booth, addressing a seminar at Reading University in 1980, revealed many discrepancies between reading ability and book choice.[9] For example, 62% of first year Juniors selected stories which were too difficult; over 97% selected information books which were too difficult. Conversely, a significant proportion of children were provided as their main readers with books which were below their ability level. There is clear need for a better match between children's reading ability and the books presented to them. Partly this is a question of book selection, but clearer book arrangement and more reading guidance by teachers are other important factors.

A catalogue is usually regarded as essential for any book collection, and it may well be that the school already has one. Here again, thought and some expert advice may save a great deal of trouble. Your catalogue can act as a check list of stock. According to its arrangement it can tell you whether the school owns a particular title, what books it has by a given author or on a specific subject. It will not tell you *where* the books are, and only a very elaborate system, recording each move to and from the central collection, will do so. Perhaps it would be better to compile a series of booklists instead of a catalogue. For example, one could make lists of books to match reading ages and interests or to link with popular projects. A catalogue needs maintaining once it has been compiled, adding cards for new stock and removing cards for worn-out books. In deciding whether or not to set up a catalogue, the staff time for keeping it up to date needs to be taken into account.

Sometimes information books are regarded as reference material which must remain in school, but fiction can usually be borrowed. Bullock found that 80% of six-year-olds in the schools surveyed were allowed to take books home. More decisions are needed in this respect, firstly about the borrowing policy, and secondly about recording method. Some schools operate the Browne system, used by many public libraries, in which each book has a card and each reader an envelope-type ticket and the two are brought together to make the loan record. Some teachers use a ruled notebook, others keep a record sheet for each child so that reading taste and progress can be monitored. R.W. Purton, in a practical manual, *Surrounded by Books*[10], describes a variety of systems, including a type of visible index showing at a glance which children in a class are borrowing books. A number of Education Library services provide schools with library stationery and can advise on the advantages and disadvantages of various loan recording systems. The choice depends mainly on whether you want to monitor where books are, or what children are reading. Any book collection needs looking after, and this can probably best be done by assigning to one teacher the responsibility for resources provision and coordination.

Whatever programmes adults devise, they must include a vital element – what is currently called 'user-education'. In the First School this is almost bound to be a continuing process. For the reception class it may mean little more than being shown where books are kept in the classroom, and becoming aware of the difference between stories and 'true books'. Children in top forms should have a familiarity with all the school's resources, be able to find and replace specific books, and understand how to extract information through index and contents pages. Wherever practicable, they should also have been introduced to the local public library. Details of such training must depend on the geography of the school, its size and organization. However, all schools, in their building up of a book policy, will need to remember to help children feel confident in finding and using books.

Stock

In planning and implementing a book policy, it is essential to know the financial framework within which it operates. Practice differs among local authorities, both in the amount of money allocated to books, and in the budget heading to which expenditure is coded. Several authorities designate a specific part of the Education Department budget to books, while others include an element for books in the standard capitation allowance. In many cases, whatever the system, the headteacher is allowed flexibility between budget heads, a practice which may serve to diminish or increase the book fund.

The National Book League[11] recommends £2.63p. per capita as a 'good' library allowance to First Schools at 1979/80 prices; £2.09p. is regarded as 'reasonable'. The Library Association[12] recommends funding adequate for provision of 11 book or audio-visual items per pupil in First Schools. If your school appears badly off in comparison there may be little to be done immediately to effect a local improvement, although longer term you can try to unite with others in putting the case for a more generous allocation. Initially, it will probably be best to seek advice from the local inspectorate, and to tap other sources, such as a Parents' Association, for funds to improve stock.

Some authorities make separate budget provision for audio-visual materials, while others expect the book budget to cover all learning resources: obviously one must be absolutely clear which system is in operation. There should be no conflict between the various types of material, for all are contributing to the same end. Many kits, indeed, recognize this unity of purpose by relating books and audio-visual materials or, as in the case of Weston Woods filmstrips, seeking to offer an extra dimension to the printed word.

Once the size of the book fund has been established, some plan for spending it needs to be drawn up, and this applies whether you are handling the fund for the whole school or only a classroom allocation. The fund has to cover newly-published titles, replacement of worn out copies, and, at least for the central collection, stock revision. Each of these categories needs separate treatment in terms of selection plans. It will probably be sensible to make a money allocation to each of these headings, and then to work out a timetable for expenditure, perhaps based on a termly buying pattern. The aids to selection of stock will vary from authority to authority, but many Education Library services have a separate display of newly published books, and all should be able to show a range of titles on favourite topics. Stock revision involves reviewing the school's stock, deciding which subjects need better coverage, and selecting books to fill the gaps. It is work which calls for a wide knowledge of children's books, and may well best be done on a cooperative basis, with other colleagues or local librarians. Book funds need managing, which implies not only selection policies and an ordering programme, but a simple system of monitoring expenditure. It is sad to see, towards the end of each financial year, teachers rushing to buy books, not necessarily the most suitable, because they have suddenly realised they still had money to spend.

Texts on book selection often speak of the need to create 'a balanced stock'. It is valuable to discuss this idea with colleagues and to work out its meaning. Are we looking for balance between the needs of various age and ability-groups in the school? The answer is likely to be 'Yes'. Are we trying to achieve a balance between information books and imaginative literature? Probably, but where to strike the balance is hard to determine. The Bullock Report concluded that 'narrative books are substantially outnumbered by non-fiction in most primary schools' and emphasized the value of literature, but neither the Report nor other authoritative works give a recommendation on the relative percentages of fiction and non-fiction which should be stocked. Some advice suggests an equal proportion of each, but at First School level, where it is sometimes difficult to differentiate between the two forms, it is probably best to consider how far the stock provided meets children's needs and forwards the school's policies, rather than worrying too much about the rather academic ideal of a balanced stock. Indeed, as far as non-fiction is concerned, one may do more good by deliberately building up an unbalanced stock, providing an in-depth collection on a limited number of subjects in demand rather than giving token coverage to each subject.

Some schools will want to set down advice on book selection, perhaps as part of a document on book policy. Here are some informal notes produced by one organization:

Book selection guidelines

1   Books are for use.
    You are choosing stock for a working collection, to be used as an important educational resource.
    Select books which you have confidence will:
    i   serve as efficient sources of information
    ii stimulate or widen interest
    iii encourage positive attitudes to books and reading
    iv assist language development
    v   develop understanding of other people
    vi help children better understand their own nature and circumstances.
2   Selection requires professional application.
    i   Base selection on either examination or knowledge of a book.
    ii Do not order from catalogues in the hope that you are making a wise choice.
    iii Do not be afraid of admitting ignorance. None of us can recall every children's book in print.
    iv Build up, in consultation with colleagues, criteria for assessing different types of book.
    v   Test your own judgment regularly against reviews and the reactions of children.
3   Stock acquisition should be linked with stock exploitation.
    Selection is only the first stage in the process of getting books read. Do not be content with choosing books and getting them into stock: work out ways of encouraging their use.

A book programme

The experience of the past decade has shown that surrounding children with books is not enough. We must prepare programmes which direct children to those books and make the use of books an integral part of the school day. As Keith Gardner has commented, reading has been regarded too much as a recognition skill. Our real objective should be to create situations where an appreciation of the uses of reading can emerge. On a very obvious level, we need to give time at school for children to read, and provide sufficient space and quiet for them to sustain concentration. If we recognise reading as a continuing process, our programmes will seek to reinforce and extend decoding skills, and will therefore operate all the way through First School. Reading as a life-long process requires stimulus from a wide range of experiences. Particularly for First School pupils, reading needs to be linked with direct experience to give life to the printed page and help children assimilate its information. It could really be said that a book programme which depends only on books is bound to be unsuccessful.

References

1. Clark, M. *Young Fluent Readers* (Heinemann Educational 1976)
2. Wedge, P. & Prosser, H. *Born to Fail?* (Arrow Books in association with the National Children's Bureau 1973)
3. Creber, J.W.P. *Lost for Words* (Penguin Books in association with the National Association for the Teaching of English 1972)
4. Chambers, A. *Introducing Books to Children* (Heinemann Educational 1973)
5. Morris, J.M. *Standards and Progress in Reading* (Slough [Berks] National Foundation for Educational Research 1966)
6. Dean, J. *Room to Learn: Language Areas* (Evans 1972)
7. Dean, J. *Room to Learn: Display* (Evans 1973)
8. Moon, C. *Individualised Reading* 5th edn (Reading [Berks], University of Reading, Centre for the teaching of reading 1975)
9. Southgate, V., Arnold, H. and Johnson, S. *Extending Beginning Reading* (Heinemann Educational 1981)
10. Purton, R.W. *Surrounded by Books* (Ward Lock Educational 1970)
11. National Book League *Books for Schools* (National Book League 1979)
12. Library Association *Library Resource Provision in Schools: Guidelines and Recommendations* (Library Association 1977)

Sources of help for the teacher

The School Library Association (Victoria House, 29–31 George Street, Oxford) is a source of advice and information. Some of its publications on library planning are now out of print, but still available is:
The Library in the Primary School 2nd edn 1966
A report of the Association's Primary Schools' Sub-committee, which gives practical guidance on equipping and running a library.

Worth looking at although slightly dated, is:
The Library in the Junior School
A teacher's guide to the planning and everday running of the primary school library, by Michael Pollard. Schoolmaster Publishing Company, 1968.

There is so much change in availability of furniture designs that there is little value in listing specific items. Both the local Education Library service and Supplies Department can provide information on current designs, and addresses of manufacturers.

A specialist firm which issues frequently updated catalogues of library equipment and furniture is:

Don Gresswell Ltd., Bridge House, Grange Park, London N21 1RB.

Joan Dean lists in her *Room to Learn series* (Evans) the sources of materials and equipment illustrated, but already some of these are no longer available.

8

Encouragements to reading

Contents

Carriers of enthusiasm
Expanding the repertoire
The reader's response

Group experiences
References

Carriers of enthusiasm

Looking at the beautiful picture books published each year, one is tempted to imagine that children will automatically be won over by their attractions, and so wooed to reading. Such, unfortunately, is not the case, as we know from statistics of the high number of children who spend little or none of their free time in reading. There is no simple formula for reversing this trend. Over the past decade there has been increased communication between the specialism of reading and related disciplines, with insights fed into the field of education by linguistic science, sociology, philosophy and the comparatively new study of psycholinguistics. Continuing research into the reading process has brought a realization that reading success depends on a complexity of factors; one cannot isolate one element in reading development as being all-important. We edge forward by attention to a range of factors.

We can, for example, create an informal and attractive physical environment which helps children feel at ease in the world of books. We can design work programmes which get children into the habit of turning to books as sources of information and pleasure. We can ensure that there are plenty of books in our library corners which inexperienced readers will not find daunting, and – the other side of the coin – plenty which able readers will not find boring. Through personal attention we can build up the confidence which is so often lacking, and give encouragement to further effort.

Often research findings can be used to illuminate classroom practice. The more we understand about the way in which children learn, the more effective we can be in promoting reading. For example, several studies have shown the link between a child's self-image and his reading growth, with improvement in the one making for progress in the other. Many specialists have emphasized the need to give children who are not established readers plenty of practice with texts which are undemanding. These bring a sense of achievement which helps to build favourable attitudes to books. Even when decoding presents few problems, we should not expect a steady line of development. As Bruner[1] has noted, the growth of intellect is not smooth but 'moves forwards in spurts'. Children may suddenly forge ahead at times, have periods of quiescence, and even regress under strain. Throughout these changes the teacher should be ready with support in these crucial First School years. The early years tend to set the pattern for all that follows. Cutforth and Battersby[2] suggest that 'a child's whole attitude to books is largely conditioned before leaving the infant school', a finding in line with those of Joyce Morris[3].

The Bullock Report cited teacher influence and book provision as the two key factors for improvement in reading standards, and it is clear that the two are closely linked. Yet, however important an attractive and adequate book stock is for the encouragement of reading, probably even more vital is the presence of an adult who can direct children to the books they are likely to enjoy, and which will give opportunities for success. As Bettina Hurlimann[4] believes: 'a child does not require too much in the way of books. What he does need are the right books at the right time'. All readers know the effectiveness of personal recommendation, but it is especially important in the early stages of reading, when knowledge of authors is limited and a wrong choice can have very discouraging results.

Reading advice begins with getting to know the reader, finding out what he already likes, accepting his current enthusiasms, and taking care not to demolish these through one's own perception of literary quality. Being a reader, says Margaret Meek[5], means operating on a deposit of satisfaction. Discrimination is a post-First School characteristic; what our counselling should reinforce in this early stage is the primacy of pleasure. Let us observe the features which children most enjoy, the humour, the domestic links, the tall stories, the rhythms and visual enjoyments, and make sure these satisfactions are available in the books we introduce. Above all, we need to keep our own delight in stories alive, so that children get caught up in our enthusiasm. Reading, said Edward Blishen[6], is a contagion and we should arrange as many carriers as possible. There is no substitute for the personal intermediary, linking text and reader.

Expanding the repertoire

As the adult intermediaries introducing children to the world of books, we must be concerned with expanding both the children's repertoire and our own.

How do we lead children towards some progression in reading choice? The first task is to establish a base of confidence from which they can explore, and this means providing books which are within children's capabilities and enjoyment level. Publishers have still not learnt the lessons implicit in the success of comics; their ease of access, ease of reading, continous action and copious illustrations are all factors which help the inexperienced reader. There are far too few books published each year which are within the experience of children at the beginning of First School; too few exciting stories which match the outside school interests of those at the top of the school. This is why the Rosens[7] advocate using some of the children's dictated stories, appropriately illustrated and presented, for in this way children can meet their own language and ideas in written form. Once children have accepted the book world as relevant for them, we can begin to extend their range. Childhood is essentially a time of experimentation when tastes change quickly, and we have a responsibility to introduce many different types of books before reading tastes are formed. Children, as M.M. Lewis[8] noted, 'are influenced considerably by the linguistic communities in which they move', and we should therefore try to make the classroom reading environment rich and varied.

In providing the opportunity and encouragement for moving forward, we have to realize that the pace of that movement will be different for each individual child. Part of the secret of enabling children to read independently is to use books which increase in difficulty very gradually and reinforce their existing knowledge. Often children will want to read the same story again and again, an indication that they want the particular satisfaction it offers. This is quite a usual pattern, and it would be foolish of us to let a belief in academic progress prevent children from finding the emotional release they seek from favourite stories. Nor, in searching out the best of each season's new publications, should we fail to give children access to books which have become accepted nursery classics, and which are always new to each fresh group of readers.

The Library Association[9] reccommends that in First Schools there should be a total of eleven books and audio-visual items per pupil, with a minimum stock of 2,640. Of these, five items 'are assumed to be in simultaneous use by each pupil'. From these figures, we can expect that there should be at least three books per head available for immediate use in the classroom. Judging from the findings on book expenditure, the average book collection in First School classrooms is likely to fall short of this level. Often the books which are available are worn and outdated; frequently their selection appears to have been haphazard. Joyce Morris has drawn attention to the close association between reading attainment and the class reading environment, and criticized the poor selection and supply of books as contributing to the difficulties of retarded readers. We cannot encourage reading when the book collection looks discouraging, and reading can hardly be regarded as a prestige activity if the library is a depressed area.

Ways of improving policy and finance have already been discussed, but these presuppose teachers who care what is on the bookshelves. Like reading, this caring is a continuous process. The teacher running on a repertoire of stories gathered in college days will eventually run out of enthusiasm. In any job there is a danger of growing stale, and we have to take positive steps to prevent it. Here British teachers and librarians inevitably envy American colleagues who have greater support in the form of book guides and bibliographies. See, for example, the predominance of American publications in the annotated bibliography, *Books about Children's Books*[10], or the comprehensive guide to children's fiction and non-fiction, *The Best of Book Bonanza*[11]. The British teacher will rely for similar advice mainly on the material issued by the Library Association, the National Book League, and the School Library Association, all of whom produce lists of their publications.

While booklists, exhibitions, libraries and bookshops all provide a way of discovering more about books, most of us need also the discipline and stimulus of other opinions. Many authorities provide opportunities for joining study groups or seminars on new books. In some cases librarians are free to come to school to introduce recent publications. If no groups exist in your area you can ask the local inspectorate or the Education Library service for some to be started. In study groups each member makes new discoveries, and benefits from other people's recommendations.

The reader's response

In Chapter One the Bullock Report's identification of three major reading stages was noted[12]. The first stage was defined as a simple decoding of the words on the page; the second as a response to the author's meaning; and the third as an engagement with the text, in which the reader's own experience and judgment are brought to bear. We, as adults, know the satisfaction of reading at this third level, and should be trying to move children towards it. The view of reading as an active involvement with text and picture has gained wide acceptance in the years since Bullock, and the subject has aroused the interest of many different disciplines, including psychology, psycholinguistics and literary criticism. Yet, strangely, although we can find article upon article stressing the need to encourage reader response, there is relatively little guidance on how to develop it.

What we find from these printed sources is a series of clues rather than a definitive programme. Most state that it is important to get children talking about the books they have read, for it is through talk that the reader consolidates – even extends – his impression of the text. Pat D'Arcy, who devotes one volume of her *Reading for Meaning*[13] to the subject of reader response, reminds us that a good book stock is essential if this kind of work is undertaken. 'Reading response at the post-decoding stage can best be developed by the provision of a wide range of literature, combined with the encouragement in school of plenty of non-directed discussion.' Other writers concentrate on making us more sensitive to the reader's reactions. They emphasize the reflective element in response, and urge us to give time for the story to make its impact. Their ideas challenge the old ideal of the 'good' reader as someone voraciously devouring print. Of course, at some stages it is desirable to get children through books quickly, for this builds up their competence and confidence. However, once these are achieved, it is better for books to be received as experiences, rather than marked up as scores in a reading race.

American specialists have long been interested in the concept of reading growth, and have made some attempt at identifying a hierarchy of response. Gray and Rogers' influential book, *Maturity in Reading*[14], provides a model showing progression from superficial to more complex responses. A more recent framework is that presented by Helen Huus[15], of the University of Missouri, in 1971. She identified a range of 'meaning levels' which included:

1 Literal or fact comprehension: this enables the reader to tell what the book says, to repeat or paraphrase the content.

2 Interpretation: this requires the reader to work out ideas not stated, to fill in the gaps in order to gain the meaning intended by the author.

3 Evaluation: judging the merit of the book in terms of theme, plot, accuracy etc.

4 Reaction: reaction, both emotional and intellectual, in terms of how the book makes one feel.

5 Integration: assimilation of the author's ideas and integration with the reader's previous ideas.

Michael Benton, writing in 1979 on 'Children's responses to stories'[16], called the subject of reader response 'the Loch Ness Monster of literary studies'. He observed that when we set out to capture it 'we cannot even be sure that it is there at all, and if we assume that it is, we must admit that the most sensitive probing with the most sophisticated instruments has so far succeeded only in producing pictures of dubious authenticity'. In the circumstances there is no need for the practising teacher or librarian to be discouraged by the experts. In this particular field there are no definitive statements. We can feel free to use other people's findings as a stimulus to our own thinking rather than as rules. The main point to take away is that if we wish to help children respond to books, we must recognize the different kinds of response possible, and their relative value to children. Only then can we help children move from simple to more complex forms. Our own work will provide examples of the range of response, once we know what we are looking for.

The reader's response is being discussed here, deliberately, in the context of 'Encouragements to reading'. We need to keep it firmly in that context. Once stories are seen merely as sources of comprehension exercises or school work we are on a course to discouraging reading. It is a matter of nice balance on a tightrope; the academic analysis of response must be applied with tact and a sense of proportion, or we move from guiding growth in reading to a rigidity which looks ridiculous when applied to First School books and readers. As Doris Young[17] in her article asks: 'How, pray, do we measure the light in the eyes that dawns during the reading of *Charlotte's Web* or *Rosie's Walk?*'.

Group experiences

'Do we have to write about it, Miss?'. That is the question which kills many potentially enjoyable school experiences. It is an indication that we need far more variety in our approach. In searching for more subtle methods we can get clues from our own reaction to books. Sometimes, when we read a story, we want to do no more than think about it or go on living in its atmosphere. It is a private experience. Children, too, are entitled to their silences, and anyone unconvinced of this would do well to read Russell Hoban's article[18], 'Teacher, be good'. 'The inside of the head is a private place . . . It takes time and experience to learn the ways of that strange instrument that can never measure itself, that strange place that can never be mapped . . . A child needs to get used to living in his mind and wandering at all levels in its private lights and darks. Not everything is to be brought out for display'.

Again, as adults we can recall occasions when we longed to be able to talk over a book just read with a friend. As social beings, much of our enjoyment and growth as individuals comes from interaction with other people. As children shed their egocentricity in their progress through the First School and become more conscious of social groups, we can capitalize on this desire to be one of a group. At the simplest level we can give children the experience of browsing among books together, and the opportunity to choose in company. We can take them to book exhibitions and arrange displays in school. We can assemble the new library books each term and talk about the stories and receive children's comments as a preliminary to reading them. By the top of the First School the peer group influence has strengthened, and we still find that, rightly handled, the children can carry much of the work of spreading enthusiasm which, in earlier years, devolved entirely on the teacher.

From the sharing of books, and the opportunity to verbalize that experience, will come a significant development in language. John Dixon's comment[19] holds true: 'Language is learnt in operation, not in dummy runs'. Discussion with adults and siblings of the experience of a story will help children understand and modify their own reaction, as well as encouraging them to relate the events and characters of the book to things they already know. 'My Dad goes on like that when I say I'm hungry'; 'That's just what happened to me when I wanted a dog'; 'I get frightened like that, so my Mum lets me have a little torch by my bed'. From the anecdotal to the revealing, the children add their contribution. This is the area particularly important to those who direct their work with books to Dixon's personal development model. Pat D'Arcy makes it clear that 'if the refinement of our social responses is to depend to some extent at any rate upon the sharpening of our insights through literature, then the encouragement that we give to children to read books must be seen not simply as a way of influencing their leisure pursuits but, more fundamentally, as a way of influencing their development as human beings'. Reading, far from being the escape of the misfit, develops best when constantly nourished by experiences from the real world.

From a teacher's viewpoint, this means the ability to produce the story which fits a real life incident, and encouragement to children to relate their world to that of the book. This kind of interchange is likely to be mainly oral, but occasionally the children will react to the book in writing, perhaps making up more about some of the characters, finding an alternative ending, or creating a fresh story. Very often the children will want to go on to paint or draw scenes from the book. Sometimes the story can be given a musical accompaniment – perhaps just for the refrain or at key action points. A very effective way of helping children internalize the experience of a story is by fairly informal drama sessions. For these, stories with a strong plot line and plenty of action are best. Through a range of creative activities children can formulate their own ideas and share imaginatively in the triumphs and troubles of other people. The block between book and life is diminished, as children engage both with the text and with one another. Today we have passed beyond the level of passive understanding achieved through comprehension exercises to an active response involving the whole child.

References

1. Bruner, J.S. 'The course of cognitive growth', *American Psychologist*, 19 (1964) 1–15.
   Reprinted in *Language in Education* (Routledge in association with the Open University Press 1972)
2. Cutforth J. & Battersby, S.H. *Children and Books* 2nd edn (Blackwell 1962)
3. Morris J.M. *Standards and Progress in Reading* (Slough [Berks], National Foundation for Educational Research 1966)

4. Hurlimann, B. *Picture-Book World* (Oxford University Press 1968)
5. Meek, M. Unpublished lecture, Berkshire, 1975.
6. Blishen, E. Unpublished interview, Reading, 1979.
7. Rosen, C. & H. *The Language of Primary School Children* (Penguin Education 1973)
8. Lewis, M.M. *Language and the Child* (Slough [Berks], National Foundation for Educational Research 1969)
9. Library Association. *Library Resource Provision in Schools: Guidelines and Recommendations* (Library Association 1977)
10. White, V.L. & Schulte, E.S. *Books and Children's Books* (Newark [Delaware], International Reading Association 1979)
11. Hopkins, L.B. *The Best of Book Bonanza* (New York, Holt Rinehart & Winston 1980)
12. Department of Education & Science. *A Language for Life* Bullock Report (HMSO 1975)
13. D'Arcy, P. *Reading for Meaning* Vol 2 *The Reader's Response* (Hutchinson Educational 1973)
14. Gray, W.S. & Rogers, B. *Maturity in Reading* (Chicago, University of Chicago Press 1956)
15. Huus, H. 'Improving children's comprehension through appropriate questioning' in Southgate, V. (Ed) *Literacy at All Levels* (Ward Lock Educational 1972)
16. Benton, M. 'Children's responses to stories', *Children's Literature in Education*, 10 (Summer 1979) 68–85.
17. Young, D. 'Evaluation of children's responses to literature', *Library Quarterly*, 37 (Jan 1967) 100–7.
18. Hoban, R. 'Teacher, be good', *The Times Educational Supplement* (21 May 1976) 6.
19. Dixon, J. *Growth through English* 3rd edn (Oxford University Press for NATE 1975)

9

Storytelling

Contents

A chance to share

Choosing the story

Presentation methods

Preparing the story

The audience

Sources for storytellers

References

A chance to share

Although we are constantly hearing that storytelling is a neglected art, there is a surprisingly large amount of printed advice on the subject, dating from the Edwardian period to our own. Each writer presents an apologia for the art, and it is fascinating to see the change over the years. Marie Shedlock[1], writing in 1915, is very conscious of the moral value of stories. Ruth Sawyer[2] in the 1940s emphasized the antiquity of the tradition and its place in folk art. Joan Cass[3] and Eileen Colwell[4] speak of 'magic' and 'delight', and 1979 finds us considering 'language-audio stimulus', the therapeutic effect, and the assistance of stories in promoting a multi-racial society[5]. All these attributes and more can be claimed. Most of them relate not to the value of telling but to the value of stories themselves, a subject discussed earlier in this book, and one on which each of us has to have a working view. If we do not believe in the power of stories, whether to assist language development, entry into a cultural heritage, personal growth or some other desirable objective, then there will be no point in spending time telling them.

Given that we do see imaginative literature as a valid and valuable part of education, what is special about storytelling? Perhaps the first point to concede is that it is a characteristic of human society which has been with us so long that it is now almost a human attribute. Its origins are with primitive man and the beginnings of language; it flourished in the minstrel's ballad, the pilgrim's tale, the courtier's gossip, and it survives today in family anecdote, coffee-table confidences and bar-side stories. Our mental construct of our own lives fits within the story mode, and this truth becomes particularly apparent when we watch young children. Children, explains James Moffett[6], 'must, for a long time make narrative do for all. They utter themselves almost entirely through stories – real or invented – and they apprehend what others say through story'. The antiquity of the tradition means that even now storytelling has overtones of ritual, mystery and myth. There is a power here which we recognize even if we cannot analyse it, and when Ruth Sawyer traces links between storytellers and priests we see this immediately as a natural progression.

Storytelling is the simple bridge between the old oral tradition and our bookish culture. Many children, as we have already noted, come to school without an acquaintance with books and one of our early tasks is to help them move towards the form and language of books. 'Lifting the print off the page', as Aidan Chambers[7] puts it, with our voice is one of the most effective ways of doing so. Eventually children will carry our range of expression into their silent reading, but until such perception is established we blur the transition from voice to print by showing the text and pictures from which our stories come. Gradually children will understand that print pins down the words into a form that can be recalled exactly, and which will be the same however many times we return to it. In a reverse but similar process children bring us their stories or news, and we record their telling in a written form which can be kept and read by others.

In our story sessions, too, we are giving practice in that most neglected of language arts, listening, and encouraging the concentration and attention which will be so valuable in many other aspects of school work. It is a great achievement when children can construct, out of sounds in the air which vanish as they are spoken, the sequence of characters and events which make up a story. As the Bullock Report[8] reminds us, we have a responsibility to introduce children to a range of language modes, from the homely and colloquial to the high style of poetry and myth. In no way can we effect that introduction better than through oral presentation.

Tellings and readings can also act as trailers for books which we hope children will go on to read for themselves. Time and again, in thinking about children and books, we come back to the value of the personal link, the need for an adult intermediary who will give the child confidence that a certain book holds satisfactions worth having. Bullock found nothing more persuasive than the personal introduction, and it is, in fact, the best means of promoting books and encouraging reading. It is significant that the best-selling titles in school bookshops are so often the ones teachers are reading in class. The reading reveals the meaning of a story in a way children are unlikely to discover by themselves. Once the adult has helped them picture characters, settings and events by the expressive use of the voice, the children can carry these memories into their own reading, and begin to develop a sense of the cadences and structures of written language.

Through such sessions reading becomes a social instead of a solitary occupation. We gather children for a shared experience – shared with us and with one another. Watch any group listening to a story or similar presentation, and you will see that laughter, excitement and emotion grow when they are met in company. Here is the 'group-generated enchantment' applauded by Jones and Mulford.[9] What would have raised a smile in a private reading becomes a cause of great merriment as children laugh both at the joke and at other people's enjoyment of it. As a class lives through a story together it becomes a virtual experience, with all the implications for change and development that the term suggests. Sharing requires a relationship of trust and friendliness, and the pleasure of a story shared goes a long way to compensate for some of the difficulties any school day brings. It is because of this requirement that visiting storytellers may be a disappointment. Sharing stories arises naturally in the familiar group, and may well have an artificiality among strangers.

Choosing the story

Among all the thousands of stories in the world, there will be some that are just right for our needs and our first concern must be to discover these. What is entailed here? Wide reading is, of course, helpful and we should always be seeking to add to our repertoire. But initially it is probably better to have a basic stock of stories in which we have confidence than a large number to which we are only half-committed. The key factors are the belief that the story is worth sharing, and the desire to share it, both highly individual matters. You have to find a story which both appeals to you and is suited to your style of delivery. Try, in private practising sessions, to work out the kind of background which suits you best. Is it King Arthur or Lone Arthur, poetry or peasant-style philosophy, action or sentiment? Are you better with the foolishness of Clever Elsa, the mystery of Rapunzel or the cunning of Brer Rabbit? Finding the answers will develop an understanding of one's own strengths and a sensitivity to the atmosphere of each story.

There are no rules about suitable material that cannot be broken. Sentimentality is generally to be avoided, but there are some people who get perilously near the edge – in some of the nativity legends, for example – without striking a false note. Gruesome stories are usually not recommended for the young, but there are enthusiasts who can read 'The Wolf and the Seven Little Kids' or 'The Story of Horace' with such aplomb that the disturbing elements are forgotten.

Special selection problems are presented in schools where children are vertically grouped, for it is difficult to find stories which will appeal to such a wide age range. Sometimes it may be possible to alter the structure temporarily so that children of the same age are brought together for stories. Sometimes we may direct the stories just to one group in the class, while the rest are occupied with other activities. The problem is one that confronts public librarians at any story programme, and which is usually overcome by offering a number of fairly short items, so that each child should find at least one absolutely suitable piece. It would be unfortunate to make too much of age-matching. In school assembly teachers regularly face the task of finding a subject or story which will have relevance to all the children, and grow to realize that even a simple story well-told can appeal to a wide age-range, each interpreting it at a different level.

Presentation methods

Having chosen a story, there are a variety of presentation methods open to us. We can tell the story, we can read it; we can show the pictures and give a linking commentary on them, or we can use an audio-visual approach with filmstrips and cassettes. The nature of the material will largely determine the method. For example, it would be sad for children to lose the unique flavour of the style of Kipling, De la Mare, Potter or Milne, and there is a strong case for leaving their texts unchanged. If a book's impact is principally visual, then it is the pictures we must present rather than the text. Where folk tales are concerned, the essence of the story is the plot line, not the style; they have developed from the oral tradition and accordingly are usually better told than read. The difference between storytelling and reading has been graphically described by Jean-Paul Sartre in *Words*[10]. 'Anne-Marie made me sit down in front of her, on my little chair; she leant over, lowered her eyes and went to sleep. From this mask-like face issued a plaster voice. I grew bewildered: who was talking? about what? and to whom? My mother had disappeared: not a smile or trace of complicity. I was an exile. And then I did not recognize the language . . . These words were obviously not meant for me. The tale itself was in its Sunday best.' How different from the familiar rendering , where the story was secondary, linked with the boy's morning bath, delivered in half-completed sentences. 'All the while she was talking, we were alone . . . two does in the wood, with those other does, the Fairies.'

Storytelling gives one a freedom to condense or expand the narrative, and a close audience rapport. While the support of the printed book is missing, so are its restrictive attributes. It is easy to adjust the vocabulary or sentence construction according to the type of listener, and to alter the pace to fit audience reaction. Class control is clearly simpler since the barrier of the book is removed and eye contact maintained. One disadvantage of storytelling is that it limits the children to our language patterns, while the story read is likely to have a richer vocabulary, more carefully balanced sentences and greater literary style. The objective of introducing children to a range of language modes does carry an implication that a number of the stories introduced in class will be read.

In many of the books for First School children illustration will play an important part, and we have to devise a way of presenting these picture books. Unless the group of children is small, it is probably best to concentrate on pictures and text separately, perhaps talking about the pictures and showing some, then reading or telling the story, and subsequently leaving the book at hand for the children to look at by themselves. Whatever methods we use, it would be a pity to feel any conflict between the various ways of presenting stories. There is a place for each, indeed one session may include a mixture of poems and stories and employ a range of presentation methods.

Whether we tell or read, the basic instrument is the same – our voice – and the value of fitting it for the purpose cannot be over-estimated. Correct breath control is fundamental to voice production, affecting tone and phrasing; once we can make the voice dependent on the breath rather than the throat we have learnt the secret. The importance of voice production for teachers and librarians is becoming more widely recognized and many professional courses include training sessions on the subject. Help is also available through a number of simple manuals and there are often opportunities to join local courses. But even without specialized advice, we can do a great deal to improve our performance, for example, by becoming aware of the sounds we make and sensitive to ways in which pitch and modulation can be improved by a conscious effort to improve range. Listening to tapes of our own readings is particularly revealing, enabling us to identify basic characteristics and analyse weaknesses.

As well as trying to make the voice more flexible, so that it can convey a wide emotional range and have the variety of tone which keeps audience interest, we can also pay attention to the clarity of our speech. Do we speak clearly; do we drop the voice at key points so that parts of words and sentences are lost; have we so pronounced an accent that we cannot be understood? Again, the use of tapes will help us pinpoint habits and mannerisms which make difficulties for the audience.

Preparing the story

Having chosen the story you will already have some familiarity with it, but this is unlikely to be enough for its presentation to an audience. At an early stage you will need to decide the overall mood or atmosphere of the story, the effect it is designed to create. The romantic pathos of 'Cinderella', the robust trickery of 'Fin McCoul', the exciting pace of 'Jack and the Beanstalk', the whimsical humour of Pooh – each requires its own pace and tone. Next we should look at the shape of the story. Children cannot take in a complex plot through the ear, so we may have to clear away sub-plot details or digressions to make the sequence of events easy to follow. There must, of course, be limits to such adaptation: if the story needs major change that is an indication that it is a wrong choice for the purpose. The plot survey will also reveal which are the high points of the narrative and the climax of the action so that we can tell where to build up emphasis and tension.

If you are telling the story there are many ways of fixing the narrative in your mind, and you will need to experiment to find a method effective for you. A large number of librarians are trained to follow the techniques advocated by two famous exponents, Ruth Sawyer and Eileen Colwell. Both recommend the method of building up the story as a series of pictures or scenes which the storyteller describes. This immediately challenges both our imagination and vocabulary. How vividly do we see what our words describe? It is worthwhile trying a few exercises to improve the colour and depth of our description. Let us try to get into sharp focus the kitchen where Cinderella spent so many hours, the little house that Goldilocks found, the cave where the forty thieves kept their treasure. Once we can see the pictures we need to pay attention to the best way in which to describe them; some stories require a rich and glamorous, even poetic, treatment while others benefit most from a spare style.

Some storytellers learn their stories by heart, but this is really a departure from the tradition. Learning by heart immediately deprives us of the spontaneity and flexibility which are among the advantages of telling. It is better to impress the story pattern rather than the exact words in the mind, reading through several times and then going through it aloud. This practice aloud is essential for it helps decision on pace and tone. There are just a few things which it is useful to get by heart – the opening and closing sentences and any refrain or repeated phrases. The opening of the story is of particular importance. Young children have a short span of attention, and the first few sentences should be planned to catch their attention and interest.

The audience

When we are sharing stories with just a few children they have easy access to the book, if we are using one, and we have the opportunity to develop a close rapport with our listeners. Hopefully, some occasions like this will occur during the school week, but for most of the time we are likely to be dealing with a whole class. Sometimes, in assembly, for example, or at a special festival, we may be addressing the whole school. Much the same advice applies whatever the size of audience. Before beginning the story, make sure you give yourself time to feel at home with your audience and give them time to adjust to you. There should be a feeling of pleasure in meeting to share an enjoyable experience. If the story is likely to be unknown it is sensible to say a little about the setting or theme, and introduce any unusual terms. Once the story has begun we want as little distraction as possible, so it is best if children's questions or comments can wait to the end, except in very small informal groups. Rhetorical questions from the story-teller are not to be recommended, for they upset the flow of the story, disturb the behaviour of the group, and lead to expectations difficult to fulfil. There is a classic anecdote of a storyteller seeking to raise interest by asking, 'And what do you think he saw then?' After the children had guessed a dragon, a giant and a witch, the right answer, a little white kitten, was hardly received with much interest.

The timing of story sessions must depend on individual teaching style and the kind of class atmosphere that is encouraged. One advantage of having a repertoire of poems and stories is that we can call on them at short notice, to link with some classroom incident or comment, or just to occupy unexpected spare time. For the timeta-bled story-time we shall probably need to build a programme, which may be based on a single theme or planned to give variety of mood and subject. Whatever the occasion, we should not mistake storytelling for a theatrical performance. Some of the most famous exponents give under-stated rather than dramatic performances, with small gestures and few distracting movements, letting the tale speak for itself. How far a different voice should be used to portray each character depends mainly on individual ability. Some variety does help to establish the characters and adds interest, but too much can become embarrassing, especially if not well done. The BBC story programmes offer an appropriate model. Where we tell stories must depend on local circumstances, but we should aim to have the children sitting com-fortably and informally where we can see them all.

Sources for storytellers

Any list immediately limits selection and encourages us to forget that new suitable titles are being published every day. There are, in any case, more lists already published than any one teacher or librarian is likely to absorb. The books listed below either guide you to some of these existing suggestions or provide material for workshop sessions.

Advice on storytelling

The classic works are:
The Art of the Storyteller by Marie L. Shedlock (New York, Dover
   Publications 1951)
Originally published in 1915, this is now available in the third edition
of 1951, with a new bibliography by Eulalie Steinmetz. The first
section of the book contains very practical advice still valid today, and
the second section has the text of eighteen of Marie Shedlock's
favourite stories.

The revised bibliography contains lists of recommended stories,
each with a brief annotation and grouped in useful sections, eg. The
folk tale, Myth and legend, Stories of the saints. The editions noted in
the bibliography are all American, but most of the stories can be
traced in British editions.
The Way of the Storyteller by Ruth Sawyer (New York, Viking Press
   1942. English ed, Bodley Head 1966)
Largely an account of Ruth Sawyer's storytelling experiences, and to
that extent inspirational rather than informational, being a wonderful
book for giving back a belief in the power of storytelling.

Eleven of Ruth Sawyer's versions of folk tales are included, and
there is a generous bibliography of stories and poems. Again, publishers noted are American, but a high proportion of the works are
available in British editions.

Joan Cass's chapters on storytelling in *Literature and the Young
Child* (Longmans, 1967) hold advice still applicable today; a more
recent view, with emphasis on classroom practice is contained in
Children and Stories, by Anthony Jones and Jane Buttrey (Oxford,
Blackwell, 1970). Both contain unannotated lists of books recommended for children of First School age, but their suitability for
telling or reading aloud is not indicated. A helpful pamphlet is
Practical Guides: Storytelling, published by the Youth Libraries Group
of the Library Association in 1979. This is a collection of papers by
experienced librarians, most of which include a list of recommended
stories. *English in Education*, in the Summer 1974 number (Vol 8, No
2) contains a wide-ranging article by Clifford Waite entitled 'Presenting stories to young children: some general principles'. This
includes advice on story selection, presentation methods and
approach, and suggestions for further activities.

Anthologies for storytellers

There are many anthologies of folk tales available, some of which are
listed in Chapter 5. The collections noted here are of stories designed
to be read aloud or told.

Fairy Gold by Ruth Ainsworth (Heinemann)
Twenty-eight favourite fairy tales in versions particularly suited to
First School audiences.
Tell me Another Story selected by Eileen Colwell (Penguin Books)
Poems as well as modern and traditional short stories, chosen for four
to six-year-olds by one of our best known storytellers. Of Eileen
Colwell's numerous anthologies, the other most-suited to First
Schools is *A Storyteller's Choice* (Bodley Head). This gives some
twenty stories and poems, many relatively unknown, with notes on
their presentation.
Stories for Six-Year-Olds edited by Sara and Stephen Corrin (Faber)
Mainly traditional tales, with a sprinkling of modern items. The plot
lines and vocabulary are within the capabilities of quite young children, and the stories read aloud without any need for alteration.
   The Corrins have produced several anthologies for different age
groups. A particularly welcome one is their volume of humorous
stories, *A Time to Laugh*, which contains modern and folk tales taken
from a wide range of sources.
The Faber Storybook edited by Kathleen Lines (Faber)
A bumper collection by a distinguished editor. Most of the stories are
fairly short, and are grouped conveniently into sections such as fables,
giant and witch stories, myths and legends, nonsense tales.
To Read and to Tell edited by Norah Montgomerie (Bodley Head)
An enthusiastic collector of nursery rhymes and tales presents here a
hundred stories drawn from old and new sources all grouped into
helpful sections.
Stories for Children edited by Anne Wood (Hodder)
A baker's dozen of stories chosen by members of the Federation of
Children's Book Groups as suited for reading aloud to mixed age
groups. This is an interesting selection of material rarely anthologized
and likely to be particularly useful at the top of the First School.

Workshop suggestions

One can, of course, base a storytelling workshop on a collection of
newly-published material, or on the titles recommended in the standard books listed above. The stories listed below – all tried and tested
– have been placed in three groups relating to *Dixon's three models*
(skills, cultural heritage, personal development) and have been
chosen by the criteria implicit in these models.

Word perfect

There are some stories which demand to be read rather than told, for
each word, each sentence is perfectly placed. Among these one can
consider:

The Shrinking of Treehorn by Florence Parry Heide (Kestrel) and *The Iron Man* by Ted Hughes (Faber)

A fairly recent publishing trend has been the production of books with a short text and limited vocabulary , which form a bridge between reading schemes and full length stories. In the examples below experienced authors enter this field.

Frog and Toad Together by Arnold Lobel (World's Work, I Can Read series)

Rose in the River by Ann Thwaite. Hodder (Stepping Stones series)

The Beetle Hunt by Helen Cresswell (Kestrel, Minnows series)

The Hermit's Purple Shirt by Janet McNeill (Macmillan Education, Language in Action series)

Links with tradition

The satisfying shape of the folk tale, with its repetitive elements and inevitable ending, can be seen both in new versions of old tales and in modern stories in the old tradition.

Captain Rocco Rides to Sheffield by Frank Arthur (Chatto & Windus)

The Rabbit who Stopped the Weather by Peter Charlton (Angus & Robertson)

The Pedlar of Swaffham by Kevin Crossley-Holland (Macmillan)

The King's Birthday Cake by John Cunliffe (Deutsch)

Hidden morals

One must believe in the value of a story in order to want to share it. The following examples show that morals or points of growth can come in attractive packages, wrapped with subtlety and imagination.

Benjamin's 365 Birthdays by Judi and Ron Barrett (Kestrel)

Victoria and the Crowded Pocket by Carolyn Sloan (Kestrel)

Weather Witch by Joanna Stubbs (Deutsch)

Tim Rabbit and the Scissors by Alison Uttley from *The Adventures of No Ordinary Rabbit* (Faber)

References

1. Shedlock, L. *The Art of the Storyteller* (New York, Appleton & Co. 1915)
2. Sawyer, R. *The Way of the Storyteller* (New York, Viking Press 1942)
3. Cass, J. *Literature and the Young Child* (Longmans 1967)
4. Colwell, E. *A Storyteller's Choice* (Bodley Head 1963)
5. Youth Libraries Group *Practical Guides: Storytelling* (Birmingham, Youth Libraries Group of the Library Association 1979)
6. Moffett, J. *Teaching the Universe of Discourse* (New York, Houghton Mifflin 1968)
7. Chambers, A. *Introducing Books to Children* (Heinemann Educational 1973)

8. Department of Education & Science *A Language for Life*. Bullock Report (HMSO 1975)
9. Jones, A. & Mulford, J. (Ed) *Children Using Language* (Oxford University Press for NATE 1971)
10. Sartre, J.P. *Words* (H. Hamilton 1964)

10

Beyond school

Contents

Community school
Library networks
Professional support

The book trade
References
Sources of help

Community school

There are still some schools which see themselves as autonomous institutions run by experts who know best. It was one of these which put up a notice board near the gate with the words, 'Private. No parents beyond this point.' Such an attitude is dying, fortunately, and increasingly schools are seeing themselves as community resources, carrying out a range of social functions. They are the place for conferences, parties and meetings, a focal point in the neighbourhood where friendships are made and news exchanged. The school should give to and draw from the community, and at an early stage in its life should begin to build up contacts, with the local councillors, for example, the church leaders, the news reporters and radio station. Above all, it must be hospitable to parents.

The first contacts may be at the pre-school stage, when parents are invited to bring their young children to see the school and meet the staff. This is bound to be a time of some stress to the parent as she/he has to reassure the child, take in a series of instructions, and adjust to the school environment. The Bullock Report suggests that this initial visit be extended into a series of book-browsing and borrowing sessions, and this proposal has been followed up in several local authorities. Such visits bring teacher, child and parent together in a very informal way, help the child to get accustomed to the language mode and expectation of school, and establish reading as an important school activity.

Many schools have a Parents' Association which gives staff and parents an opportunity to know one another. It would be a pity to regard such associations only as fund-raising agencies, for that should not be their prime purpose. However, they are often a real source of help, and serious book needs should certainly be brought to the association's committee. Sometimes parents are free to come in during the day and can be asked to spend time improving the book collection's effectiveness – by colour-coding, cataloguing, or fitting plastic jackets, for example. If a clear case can be made for substantially improving the school book stock, financial assistance may be forthcoming.

Even more than cooperation in fund-raising activities, we need the parents' cooperation in supporting, by home attitudes and facilities, our work of promoting reading. The significance of home conditions was brought to our attention by Joyce Morris[1] over ten years ago in her seminal study, *Standards and Progress in Reading*, which considered the influence of both home and school conditions on children's reading. Later research has corroborated these findings. For example, Margaret Clark[2] in her community study of specific reading difficulties, found that most of the poor readers were from homes without books. Of the most severely backward readers she recorded 'little evidence of active assistance from the home. Few of these children mentioned being read to at home. . . . Reading within this group tended to be confined to "my school reading book", or "my sister's school reading book"'.

We must accept that book reading is an activity foreign to many parents. We shall need patience and tact to bring books into the culture of parents, and win their acceptance of the centrality of reading in education. Our first task must be to build up a reading environment in the school. The second has to be finding ways in which that influence can spill over into the home. The following suggestions indicate just some of the ways of doing this:

Make sure parents see books attractively displayed – in entrance lobby, corridor and classroom.

Demonstrate the link between books and school activities by displaying children's drawings, poems, project work, etc with the books which stimulated them.

Arrange book events at school to which parents and younger children are invited.

Make sure, through meetings and informal sessions, that children understand the importance of reading.

Let children borrow books to take home. One Berkshire school achieved a closer link with parents by arranging a session for borrowing books and reading games at the end of the school day. Another achieved it by opening a lending library for pre-school children.

It would be quite wrong to assume that all parents need converting to a belief in books. Many parents will already have this, and their children will come to school with a background of enjoyable reading experiences. *Young Fluent Readers*[3] contains several examples of the way schools fail to help such children. Book-oriented parents still need reading guidance, but perhaps of a more specific nature. This is where local librarians and advisory staff may be particularly helpful, in suggesting books which reconcile the gap which often exists between reading age and interest age. There is really scope here for developing the children's reading, the parents' enthusiasm, and the teachers' understanding, and there may be a case for carrying forward discussion by informal parents' sessions, either within one school or a group.

An encouraging book recommended for both the committed and uncommitted parent is *Babies Need Books* by Dorothy Butler[4], the redoubtable New Zealand teacher and book seller. It shows a sensitivity towards developmental needs, has plenty of practical ideas, and book lists for each age-group from one to six years.

Library networks

In her study *Young Fluent Readers* Margaret Clark found that more than half of these children were making use of public libraries, a link borne out by Joyce Morris's Kent survey, *Reading in the Primary School*[5], and by the Ministry of Education survey of reading standards[6], which noted thriving public library membership in schools where reading scores were high. We need to move in two directions here, encouraging pupils to join the local library, and discovering the ways in which the library can help the school. At an early stage the teacher should make contact with the local library staff, get to know them, and ascertain the services available. It is probable that the librarian will welcome visits from school parties, in which the children can get accustomed to the building and the staff, be encouraged to become members, and discover the kind of stock available. The librarian may also be free to visit school occasionally to introduce some newly-published books and perhaps tell some stories.

Your local library may be small or large, but whatever its size, it will be linked to a network of other libraries, and will be able to borrow for you books not in its stock. This is a particularly useful source for the kind of books required for professional development. There may also be specialist libraries connected with a nearby university or college which will welcome outside borrowers: your public library should be able to give you information on these additional resources.

Library work with children is taken seriously in most countries with a developed public library system, and we can find examples of service of high standard in countries as far apart as Sweden and

Australia, Scotland and Canada. The relation between these public library systems and school libraries varies considerably, as the international survey, *Library Service to Children*[7] makes clear. In England the relationship is particularly close, largely because of the pattern of local government organization. London is a special case, with school library development in the hands of the Inner London Education Authority, and public library development in the hands of the individual boroughs. In other areas of England, teachers will have access to an Education library service operated by a special section of the public library service.

Obviously, standards and facilities will vary. However, a typical service will offer a loan stock, with opportunities for exchange through regular visits of mobile libraries; a project service for short-term loans of books and audio-visual materials; and a range of advisory or promotional activities. Librarians will be available to visit school to advise on stock selection, organization, or planning of library areas. They may also be available for book talks and story sessions, or to assist in special activities such as Book Weeks. A list of suggested functions for such a service is set out in the booklet, *The Public Library Service Reorganisation and After*[8] prepared by the Department of Education and Science, but it is probably true to say that, once you have got to know the librarian covering your school, cooperation will be limited only by your joint time and imagination.

The headquarters of the Education library service will be a place you can visit to browse, to inspect new publications, or to look at exhibition collections. Often the unit will issue lists of recommended new books, or of special categories of books, or it may convene study groups of teachers and librarians which will bring out recommendations. In addition, your authority may operate a purchase scheme, by which books may be bought direct from the section's headquarters library. Most services are only too anxious to operate on lines appropriate to school needs and welcome comments or requests for assistance.

Professional support

A major source of support for any teacher must be the authority's advisory staff. They will give an assessment of your current standard of book provision and use, and offer suggestions for improvement. They are the people to consult about additional resources or training. Through in-service courses they and Education Library service staff will try to encourage discussion of the role of books in school, promote awareness of suitable titles, and assist teachers to make book collections more effective. The advisory staff also play a part in giving observations on policy, so it is to them that you should turn if you have problems or ideas relating to the authority's policies. The directors of Teachers' Centres also act as a focus for local interest, and are always seeking ways to support practice.

In many areas the difficulty may be not that of shortage of advice, but of getting to know all the agencies which are potential sources of help. Education advisers or the Education Library service staff will be able to provide information on these – which may well include a Reading Centre, an English Language Centre, informal groups, such as an English workshop, and branches of national organizations, such as the United Kingdom Reading Association and the School Library Association. The national organizations are likely to provide for corporate as well as personal membership, and most schools will benefit from joining and so enjoying the opportunity to attend meetings and receive publications. If our own thinking about our work is to expand, it is necessary to see that work in the context of national movements and not just local events.

The book trade

While teachers often take some care to establish professional links, trade contacts are frequently neglected. This is a great pity for we share many joint interests, form part of one book world, and are to a large extent interdependent. If there are shortages of material for particular age-groups or interests, it is to the publishers that we should make representation. If there are supply delays, it is to the booksellers we should turn. Local bookshops are extremely important to our work of promoting reading. It is to them that we hope children and parents will go as regular customers, and we can try to ensure that they will be encouraged not discouraged by their reception. Teachers and librarians should, as a matter of course, make themselves known to local booksellers and try to channel some business their way – the local bookseller will always be able to supply ordinary stories and information books for the school, i.e. net books. He may not be a source of supply for textbooks, i.e. non-net books. The retailing conditions for these two types of book are quite different. Net books are sold at a price fixed by the publisher, and under the Net Book Agreement shops are not permitted to sell these to schools or individuals at a discount. Non-net books are not subject to this condition and are usually sold at a discount to institutional buyers. It is common practice for Local Education Authorities to ask firms to tender for a contract for textbook supply. Sometimes contracts are awarded only to national suppliers; sometimes local booksellers may be on the approved list of textbook suppliers. The administration unit of the Education Department will be able to give information on this point.

One way to make the local bookshop familiar ground is to take some pupils along to help choose new books for the school collection. Occasionally the bookseller may be invited to arrange a book exhibition in school. Once the personal contact has been established, many ideas may follow on cooperation to mutual advantage. In Berkshire, for example, such modest beginnings have now encouraged one bookseller to open a separate children's bookroom, and another to organize an annual Book Fair, with a large exhibition, speakers, competitions, and a host of other promotional activities.

It may be that you would like to move even closer to bookselling by opening a school bookshop. There is no doubt that book ownership is related to reading progress, and many schools, realising the connection, are now operating schemes which enable children to buy books from school. These may range from a simple book club scheme, like the Puffin Club, to a bookshop in school. If you are thinking about embarking on such a project, advice should be available locally through your Education Library service, which can provide names and addresses of clubs and details of different selling methods. In some areas courses are organized on the subject, but in any case names of other schools operating bookshops should be available.

Basically, in opening a bookshop one has a choice between liaison with a local commercial bookseller, or using a national specialist organization, such as Books for Students. There are advantages and disadvantages of both. The national organization offers expertise and backup resources unlikely to be obtained locally, while the local bookshop provides a personal service and browsing facilities. In reaching a decision, it will be helpful to visit schools operating on these different bases, and hear from colleagues at first-hand their observations. The school bookshop movement may initially have been orientated towards Secondary Schools, but there are now many thriving bookshops in First Schools. The following extract from a report on an Infant School bookshop at the end of its first year of operation gives a not untypical picture: 'Sales during the year were just over £700 and the headmistress and staff were delighted with the growing response from the children, and the support and interest which was also being shown by parents.' Sometimes establishment of a school bookshop highlights the plight of children without the money to buy books, and it is sensible to run a 'Swop shop' scheme concurrently with a club or shop. There is now a national school bookshop movement and a lively journal, *Books for Keeps*, which contains book reviews, news and ideas. The movement owes much to the enthusiasm of one man, Peter Kennerley, who received the Eleanor Farjeon Award for this contribution. He emphasises that 'School bookshops happened not because publishers and booksellers wanted to sell more books, or because someone in education had a theory, but because a lot of ordinary teachers, parents and librarians wanted children to read"[9]. Two major forces, the school world and the commercial book trade, had previously pursued their interests in children's reading quite separately: they have come together with outstanding success in the school bookshop movement to promote a simple idea, the enjoyment of reading.

References

1. Morris, J.M. *Standards and Progress in Reading* (Slough [Berks], National Foundation for Educational Research 1966)
2. Clark, M. *Reading Difficulties in Schools* (Penguin Books 1970)
3. Clark, M. *Young Fluent Readers* (Heinemann Educational 1976)
4. Butler, D. *Babies Need Books* (Bodley Head 1980)
5. Morris, J.M. *Reading in the Primary School* (Newnes, for the National Foundation for Educational Research 1959)
6. Ministry of Education *Standards of Reading: 1948–1956* (HMSO 1957)
7. International Federation of Library Associations *Library Service to Children* 3 vols Vols 1 & 2 Lund (Sweden) Bibliotekstjänst 1963, 1966.
Vol 3 Copenhagen (Denmark) Bibliotekscentralen 1970.
8. Department of Education & Science *The Public Library Service: Reorganisation and After* (HMSO, 1973)
9. Kennerley, P. *Running a School Bookshop* (Ward Lock Educational 1978)

Sources of help

Although still small, there is a growing interest by parents in children's reading and approach to books.
A pioneer organization is:
The Federation of Children's Book Groups
    Secretary: Brenda Marriott,
                6 Cavendish Court, Park Road, Eccleshill, Bradford.

The Federation aims to promote awareness of and involvement in children's literature, principally among parents, and has many local branches. Associated with it is a magazine specifically designed for parents, with helpful articles, reviews and book lists:
Books for Your Children
Joint editor and subscriptions officer: Jean Russell,
                                        Slate House Farm,
                                        Parwich, Ashbourne,
                                        Derbyshire.

Parent interest has also been encouraged by the formation of family reading groups, which increase awareness of new children's literature and improve home/school/library liaison. Further information is

contained in:
How to Run Family Reading Groups by Cecilia Obrist, United Kingdom Reading Association, 1978.
Parents are best helped by personal advice and provision of books for home borrowing. For those who would like to read around the subject themselves, the following guides are recommended:
To Begin With by Eileen Colwell. Kenneth Mason, 1964.
An annotated list of books for under-fives, grouped into sensible sections. Although old, most of the books listed are still available.
Children and Books by Ann Wood. Home and School Council Publications, 1973.
One of a series designed to encourage fruitful home/school links. After an enthusiastic introduction, on the role of parents in reading development, a series of book lists follow, covering Primary school age-groups. Each title listed carries a brief annotation.

To foster professional contacts, the two following associations are recommended:
The School Library Association
    Victoria House, 29–31 George Street, Oxford.
This exists to promote the use of the school library as an instrument of education, has local branches, and publishes a journal, *The School Librarian.*
United Kingdom Reading Association
    The Hollies, 85 St. Helens Road, Ormskirk,
    Lancashire
The association's purpose is to study reading problems at all educational levels and to encourage research in reading. It is a very active association with a journal *Reading*, influential national conferences, and local branches.

An organisation which brings together all areas of the book world is:
The National Book League, now established at Book House, 45 Easthill, Wandsworth.
The League arranges many exhibitions of interest to teachers: in most cases an annotated booklist is published and the exhibitions are available for hire. Book House maintains a permanent exhibition of recently published children's books, and holds an annual 'Children's Books of the Year' exhibition. The League is active in campaigning for better book provision in schools, witness its 1979 report, *Books in Schools.*

The school bookselling movement is promoted by:
The School Bookshop Association, which is based at The National Book League, Book House, 45 Easthill, Wandsworth.
This is mainly a promotional and liaison body, which spreads ideas through its journal, *Books for Keeps.*

There are too many firms interested in selling books to schools for listing to be practicable. Books for Students, Catteshall Lane, Godalming, is a specialist firm which assists in setting up and stocking paperback bookshops in schools. Among the larger book clubs are the Puffin School Bookshop (Red House Bookshop, 93 High Street, Thame) and those operated by Scholastic Publications (Westfield Road, Southam, Leamington Spa). There are also smaller organizations, of particular regional relevance, such as Children's Book Club (Bishops Place, Paignton), and Bookworm Club (Napier Place, Cumbernauld, Glasgow).

Further information is obtainable from the National Book League. Before entering into arrangements with bookselling organizations outside your area, it advisable to visit local bookshops to ascertain what services can be provided close at hand.